If Only I Had Known

Smart College Decisions that
Pay Off Handsomely

Michael Raulin, PhD

If Only I Had Known

Smart College Decisions that
Pay Off Handsomely

Michael Raulin, PhD

Copyright

If Only I Had Known:
Smart College Decisions that Pay Off Handsomely
Michael Raulin, PhD

ISBN-13: 979-8-9859925-0-2

Copyeditor: Stacey Lenn aka Grammargal
Cover Design: Tanveer Ahmad

Table of Contents

Preface

It has been said that "youth is wasted on the young." That is a paraphrase of a longer quotation from George Bernard Shaw. This idea seems to resonate with those of us who no longer qualify as young. We think about how much better we could have managed our life and career *if only we had known*. As parents, teachers, coaches, and neighbors, we want to use the wisdom we learned over time to help younger people navigate the world more effectively.

So what do older people possess that younger people do not possess? It certainly is not a better body, more energy, or better health. Nevertheless, older individuals often make more money, and not just because they have been around longer and have accumulated more raises. They often know more, and they often set priorities more effectively. Often, the most important asset of older people is having had more time than younger people to accumulate experiences, take advantage of opportunities, and explore alternatives. I deliberately left off making mistakes from this list because most people do not consider that an advantage. But we learn from mistakes, or at least we hope we learn from them. Yesterday's mistakes are the seeds of today's wisdom.

This book is not about how some older people can compete successfully with younger people and other older people cannot. Instead, it is about how some younger people become more competitive than their peers and rise at a young age to become leaders in their fields.

Not everyone is cut out to be our traditional idea of a leader, although most people have more leadership potential than they realize. Moreover, our traditional idea of leadership fails to recognize that there are many ways in which one can be a leader. In addition, the first person to propose a good idea is not the only leader in the group. The first people to recognize a good idea and publicly support it are every bit as important in the success of the idea. In fact, without these "first supporters," great ideas may fall by the wayside. We are starting to realize the complexity and many forms of leadership, and that understanding is giving more people the chance to become leaders and to make a difference in the world.

Becoming a leader does not happen by accident, although random events are a part of everyone's developmental history. However, among the randomness of our lives are strategic decisions and actions that have the potential to change our destiny. Note the careful wording; we can do everything right to be successful and still be hit by a bus tomorrow and lose it all. Life is always a matter of chance. When we play poker, sometimes the cards go our way and we win. Other times, the cards do not go our way and we lose. However, if we play smart, we can win more often than those who rely solely on the hand they are dealt.

Playing poker is so much easier than living life; we can compute the probabilities of drawing the card(s) that we need and use that information to make decisions. Doing the same computations and making decisions for our life is much more difficult. Nevertheless, we can make better decisions if we know critical information in advance. That is the premise of this book.

Young people have tremendous advantages, including energy, health, passion, and quick recovery from those inevitable injuries. Their primary disadvantage is that they often lack the information to make the best possible decisions when those decisions must be made. Few things in life are only available to us once, but almost everything in life has an optimal time. For example, young children learn new languages much better than adults. If being bilingual is valuable, the easiest time to build that skill is in young children, not in college students or older adults. However, adults can and do learn foreign languages; it is just harder. Children can be great role models for us. They attack new things with a playful curiosity, and they are usually not afraid to ask questions. Do not be afraid to embrace your inner child as you strive to learn more.

The focus of this book is on academic decisions made from high school through graduate and professional school. It focuses on optimal strategies that many students miss, not because they are not motivated, but because they lack the knowledge or the coaching available to other equally talented students. If everyone has the same information, the playing field is level. Having information does not guarantee success, but not having information may well get in the way of success. Motivation, hard work, and drive will always be part of the success equation, and no amount of information will replace these variables. This book is aimed at those students who have the motivation and drive to succeed but not the information about how the game is played.

I am deeply indebted to several people who helped to move this project along and contributed immensely to the success of the project. My colleague, Sharon Stringer, reviewed the prospectus and made several excellent suggestions. Two of my best students (Emily Stran and Lexi Rager) reviewed the entire manuscript. They now are in graduate school or have an advanced degree, and both are well on their way to distinguished careers. Their insights were extremely helpful. I am also indebted to my copyeditor (Stacey Lenn) and cover designer (Tanveer Ahmad). With the help of all these people, I was able to make this book a better product.

Mike Raulin
MikeRaulin@gmail.com

Chapter 1
Committing to Success

It may be politically incorrect to say so, but the world is competitive. It has been competitive for millions of years, and inherent competition has shaped the evolution of species throughout the planet's history. The way we compete today is different than it was one hundred thousand years ago, when it was literally a life-and-death struggle, but we still compete. We are a species that prospers because we work together, and one of the consequences of this cooperativeness is that we provide basic services to most people. However, there is a big difference between just surviving and prospering in today's competitive and constantly changing environment.

Success is one of those concepts that is more complicated than it first appears. Some people measure success by the money one has; others measure it by the satisfaction and love within their families. Success is a personal value, and it is not my intention to tell anyone which values should guide your life. However, if success for you involves achieving certain goals in school, using those achievements to leverage good jobs, and turning those jobs into careers that provide both personal satisfaction and reasonable financial security, this book can help.

Success is not the same as winning. Winning is usually defined as being the best at something. Only one person wins the golf tournament, and one team wins the Super Bowl. But players who make a living doing what they enjoy and receive the respect of others for their work are winning in their own right. Few people ever win the Super Bowl or a Nobel or Pulitzer Prize. Nonetheless, many people enjoy satisfying and lucrative careers, even if the major prizes have eluded them. For most people, career satisfaction rests on doing something that feels worthwhile and being successful enough that one can be financially secure.

Setting Your Goals

To achieve anything consistently, you must have a clear sense of your goals so that you can direct your energy toward them. To be successful in school, you must decide on what career directions you want to take and find out what academic credentials will foster them. That choice is easier said than done. It is rare that entering college students have a solid base of information on which to make career decisions. Many students simply go into the careers they know, perhaps because those were the careers of their parents, relatives, or neighbors. Alternatively, students may select careers that feel prestigious. Still other students seek careers in fields that interest them, such as science, sales, or construction. Other students seek the advice of those they respect. And, of course, since we are typically teenagers when we are making these decisions, we sometimes make our choices because our parents specifically discouraged such choices. Hey, one of the joys of being young is rebelling!

Our sense of direction in life may come from many sources, but regardless of the source, we need a sense of direction. Moreover, we need to feel committed to our direction. For example, if you select a career based solely on the advice of others, you may find yourself feeling a lack of commitment to that decision. Ultimately, you need to take ownership of your career choices. By committing to a career goal, you can avoid wandering aimlessly without direction.

There are so many myths about the directions we take in life. For example, many people search their entire lives for their one true love. Whether that idea came from romance novels or language that includes words like *soulmate*, the concept of one true love is highly unlikely to be true. We can easily have lifelong relationships that are satisfying and rewarding with many different people. Even with the Internet, the idea of finding your perfect partner is, at best, daunting.

Similarly, people believe that there is a perfect set of life goals. Certain occupations may be more emotionally satisfying and lucrative, but if those occupations are not available, there will be other occupations that have their own rewards. The world is changing rapidly, and as a result, potential occupations open and close quickly. Sometimes potential occupations are still open, but they are no longer personally satisfying. An attitude that suggests that only one occupation can be rewarding for you paints you into a corner. Today, if you want to be successful, you should have career goals. The goals should fit your skills and your temperament. But those goals should also be flexible because career opportunities are difficult to predict. Instead of having a single career in mind, think in terms of careers that would be satisfying and effective for you.

This book addresses the issues described here in three sections. The goal is to provide a structure to understand the various elements that will give you an advantage in whatever career direction you wish to take.

Section I: The Importance of Attitudes and Strategies

Attitude is often the key to ultimate success. But the right attitude is of little value if you do not have strategies and skills to achieve your goals. The first section of the book deals with these elements. We start with a concept called a *growth mindset*, which involves a belief that one is constantly learning and improving, or at least is capable of such growth. Understanding the value of this mindset requires that you recognize the alternative (a *fixed mindset*). A fixed mindset means that you are already the person you will always be, so struggling to be more is simply frustrating and demoralizing. The truth is that growth is frustrating, but it does not have to be demoralizing. If you focus on rewarding yourself for the hard work and the improved skills that develop from that persistence, it can be invigorating.

Improving your skills in college to be more marketable involves learning; most people are unaware of the best strategies for learning. College is hard, but it does not have to be as hard as many people make it. I introduce some easily incorporated strategies that will improve the efficiency of your studying. Part of that efficiency comes from understanding and appreciating how the fundamental principles of disciplines were created and the strategies used by the pioneers to develop the field.

Michael Raulin

Finally, if you want to be successful, you need a plan. I have always been amazed at how many people believe the best plan is to wing it. Sometimes that is all you can do because the world can be unpredictable. But a flexible plan that is periodically updated to reflect changes in your situation or values can be enormously helpful in guiding your work in college and beyond.

Section II: The Keys to Academic Success

The first section of this book covers the skills and attitudes that will enhance your college success. But the goal of college is not to be successful in college. The goal of college is to prepare you for the real world or for the advanced training required for the most demanding careers. Section II addresses strategies that go beyond getting good grades in college; it covers the strategies that will make strong students even more competitive beyond college.

Although your major in college will not define your entire career, it certainly opens doors for some careers. Finding the right major is complex, and few students enter college with the knowledge and insights to make such a critical decision. Fortunately, the early years in college give you time to explore potential majors and minors and still be able to graduate within four years. Selecting your major is only one key decision; you also need to decide whether graduate or professional training is for you and how to be more competitive for those programs. This section covers those decisions and begins to focus on the ultimate decision about your career.

Section II also covers two of the most important strategies that will strengthen a student's competitiveness for advanced training or a career right out of college. The first is getting to know the right people. Universities are filled with people who want to help you succeed, but students often do not appreciate how valuable these people could be to their long-term success. Developing a strong relationship with one or more faculty members during your undergraduate education can provide critical resources for your goals. Such a relationship can teach you skills not generally covered in classes, give you insights into your potential career, and give you the sort of support and mentorship that can be the difference between a good outcome and an outstanding outcome.

The second is planning your career path, which involves extensive research on options, expectations, and opportunities. Such planning cannot wait until your senior year. You should be exploring options by your sophomore year. Your early decisions may change as your values and experiences shape your direction. Consequently, your plans will shift. That is normal and healthy. You will be surprised at how plans that you eventually discard will help you to be better at formulating the next plan.

Section III: Finding and Using Mentors

The final section covers the transition from college to graduate training to career aspirations. Much of this section deals with the way you learn when classes are behind you. Everything you learn in college is generally outdated in ten years, and what you learn in graduate or professional school is outdated in five years. Your long-term success will be built on continuing to learn new information and learning the strategies to remain on top in a world that constantly changes. Much of this focus is on the value of mentors, how to find them, how to work with them in a symbiotic manner that will advance you both, and how to transition to the role of being a mentor.

The final two chapters in this section cover a critical topic often overlooked in advice books. Success in life depends on constant work, constant growth, and dealing with constant challenges. Doing that requires a balance in your life to maintain your energy, optimism, and focus over decades. There is no single way to achieve this balance. However, there is little doubt that without such balance, success is less likely and, even if you were to achieve it, less enjoyable.

Chapter Summary

Many books help students be more successful in college, but this book is unique in that it addresses principles that start with success in college and extend the focus to success well beyond college. For many careers, such long-term success requires graduate or professional schooling, and entry into those programs is often extremely competitive. This book also covers those activities and achievements that increase a student's competitiveness for such programs. Students interested in advanced training and high-pressure careers want to be successful, and such success depends on a lot more than just good grades. Much of this book covers the attitudes, skills, and experiences critical to such success. It is my sincere hope that the information in this book will open options in your college and professional life and help you achieve the goals you set for yourself.

Section I
Developing the Right Attitude

One of my favorite quotations comes from Henry Ford, whose name is still synonymous with automobiles and trucks. Ford argued, "Whether you think you can or think you can't, you're right." Attitude is an essential ingredient to success. These next few chapters focus on what is meant by the right attitude and how one can develop and nurture it. One thing is certain: you will fail along the way. Failing is not the issue. The issue is what you do when you fail. The people we call winners are not people who win all the time. They are the ones who have learned to come back from losing, and they often come back stronger and better. We also have a distorted view of real-world losses because we are much more likely to hear about victories than losses, so we think, based on this biased sample of information, that victories are the norm and losses rarely occur.

I am a big believer in sports as a critical learning tool for young people. Sports teach you valuable attitudes, such as the importance of teamwork, the willingness to keep playing and fighting even if success is unlikely, and the ability to lose and come back another day to compete again. You can learn these attitudes in other ways, but sports teach these lessons while promoting other essential values, such as communication, cooperation, sportsmanship, and pride. Not every important lesson in life is learned in a classroom. I have spent most of my life teaching in a classroom, and I can tell you with confidence that the most important lessons in my life were learned elsewhere.

One reason I believe in sports is that it is a great way to learn how to both win and lose. Vince Lombardi, the legendary coach of the Green Bay Packers and the person for whom the Super Bowl trophy is named, once said, "Winning isn't everything; it's the only thing." Lombardi was wrong, and I say that half expecting to be struck down for such blasphemy. I grew up in Wisconsin, where being a Packers fan is almost a religious experience. I do not believe Lombardi meant it literally when he voiced that colorful quotation. He and his team lost occasionally, although they won more. He did not like losing, he did not accept losing, and he was outstanding at motivating his players to never like or accept it either. A loss is just a way to remind us how much better winning feels. However, you do not ignore losses unless you want to lose more. Instead, you learn from losses what it takes to win. Lombardi knew that, and virtually everyone with a history of success before and after the Lombardi era knew the same thing.

You will learn in this section that expecting yourself to always win is a recipe for losing, or worse, quitting. An even worse expectation is that you will always lose because that can easily become a self-fulfilling prophecy. Instead, you need the attitude that you expect yourself to succeed. Success involves winning sometimes but learning from each loss. The more you learn, the more likely it is that you will win. In chapter 2, you will learn about a concept called the *growth mindset*, which is an attitude that being smart is not an adjective to describe yourself, but rather a goal to constantly strive to achieve. You become smarter by doing the things you do not do well until you can do them well. The alternative to a growth mindset is a *fixed mindset*, in which you believe you are either smart or not smart. Working on things that you are not good at in a fixed mindset is terrifying because your inevitable failures are "proof" that you are not smart. Consequently, having a fixed mindset means you fail to grow, learn more, and fully develop your potential.

Success is built on progress and growth. Early in our careers, that primarily involves learning. In fact, in the most successful people, progress and growth continue to involve learning. We all dream of having a photographic memory (technically called an *eidetic memory*), where if you glance at a page, you remember it forever. Few people have such a memory, and frankly, it is not as helpful as one may think. Take out your cell phone and photograph each page of a textbook, and you have created a photographic memory. But to find the information you need, you must look through all those pictures just like you would have to look through the original textbook. You have not learned it. You have simply recorded it. Learning means storing the information in a way that makes it accessible to you when you need it, and learning is hard work. Chapter 3 will teach you why learning is so hard and what you can do to maximize it.

Knowing the answers is not enough; you need to be able to communicate what you know in a manner that is clear, concise, and persuasive. You likely know the basics of writing and speaking by the time you reach college, but the basics are not enough if you wish to be successful professionally. Chapter 4 covers the importance of these communication skills and several ways to improve those skills.

The most valuable information is not facts, nor is it principles. The most valuable information is how to solve problems and develop new information to guide growth and development. You learn that by focusing not just on the ideas you wish to learn but who created or discovered those ideas and how they did it. That is the focus of chapter 5.

The final attitude variable is the five-year plan, which is covered in chapter 6. Many people think of plans as restrictions that prevent them from being flexible enough to prosper. If that is your idea of a plan, you are not doing it right. Plans should not be restrictive; instead, they should lay out priorities, tentative strategies to achieve those priorities, and a process to constantly update those priorities as situations change. A five-year plan is a reasonable time horizon to chart a steady course, but no five-year plan is intended to last for five years. Good five-year plans are updated every two years or so. Sometimes the updates are minor, but often they represent a significant change due to the situation. But a good plan clarifies values that guide all decisions. Situations change, opportunities change, priorities change, but values stabilize early in one's life and can remain consistent despite all the other changes.

Overall, this first section will focus on attitudes, strategies, and procedures on which you will build your long-term success. These are tools that will serve you throughout your life and will dramatically improve your college performance.

Michael Raulin

Chapter 2
A Growth Mindset

O ne of the most intriguing concepts that has contributed to improving one's long-term performance is the concept of a growth mindset. Developed by Carol Dweck (2006), a *growth mindset* is the idea that one's abilities can and do improve over time through the process of learning. You may find that idea puzzling because it seems obvious that our abilities improve with practice and learning. What could make this concept so intriguing?

To appreciate the incredible power of a growth mindset, you need to understand the alternative position (a fixed mindset) and why many people, if not most people, accept this alternative. In a *fixed mindset*, we believe that we possess innate abilities that are both a part of being human and influenced by our genes. For example, some people are inherently more athletic and do well at many types of athletic endeavors. Others are good at math. Some have a gift for words and learn to be excellent writers. Others use words most effectively when they speak.

We refer to a generalized cognitive ability as *intelligence*. We define intelligence as the ability to learn new things quickly, to remember information, and to solve problems (White, 2006). More intelligent individuals tend to do better in school, go to college, and often earn advanced degrees. They tend to enter intellectually demanding occupations, becoming doctors, lawyers, engineers, and scientists. When they go into fields like business, they often move up quickly because they learn new skills as needed and are adept at solving problems that others cannot solve. We know that highly intelligent people tend to do well in school and often do well without working all that hard. The tasks that are part of school seem to be easier for them.

The concept of intelligence has been a part of psychology and education for more than a century, and it is also a part of our everyday set of concepts. We all know people who are intelligent and others who seem to lack those skills and so struggle more in school and beyond. The concept of intelligence is widely accepted, although skepticism about the nature of intelligence is warranted. We once believed that intelligence was a fixed aspect of the person, which is clearly present early in life and remarkably stable throughout life, but our notion of intelligence has shifted as we learned more (e.g., Benisz, Willis, & Dumont, 2018).

Some of our ideas about intelligence are true. Clearly, some people are better at solving problems or learning new skills than others. Genes do play a role in intelligence. The heritability coefficient for standard intelligence test scores is .80, which means that 80 percent of the variability in the performance on intelligence tests is a function of one's genes and 20 percent is a function of the environment. We will talk about heritability and the heritability coefficient later.

What may not be immediately obvious, but is critical to our discussion, is that the concept of intelligence represents a fixed mindset. There clearly are individual differences in these cognitive skills, they are relatively stable, and they are influenced heavily by our genetic heritage. But this simplified concept has been challenged on several fronts over the past century (Mackintosh, 2011). The idea that intelligence is a single concept that affects every area of cognitive functioning has given way to the idea that there are subtypes of intelligence, which are somewhat related but also somewhat independent of one another (Sternberg, 2015). The idea that intelligence is inborn and unchanging has also been challenged. We know that if one continues to challenge oneself to learn more, perhaps by continuing his or her education, one's performance on IQ tests improves (Warne, 2020). We also know that people who do little intellectual activity tend to show a drop in IQ test scores over time (Warner, 2013). Finally, we know that those who keep intellectually active tend to show a later onset of dementia when they have Alzheimer's disease and a slower progression of this disease (Addae, Youssef, & Stone, 2003). Essentially, this later finding represents a "use it or lose it" phenomenon found in physical health and many skills.

What contributed most to the concept of intelligence as being fixed is the strong heritability coefficient. It is perhaps one of the most misunderstood concepts in statistics. The fact that the heritability coefficient is .80 means that in our current population and our current environment, 80 percent of the variability of the IQ scores is due to genes and 20 percent to the environment. This .80 number comes from an analysis for Western cultures, such as the United States. The number may be different in other cultures with different educational systems. That .80 number is incorrectly interpreted by some people to mean that intelligence is mostly due to genes and therefore cannot be changed. That interpretation is wrong.

Let us take an example that has an even stronger genetic influence: a genetic disorder called PKU. PKU is the result of a single recessive gene. If you have one copy of the gene, you are fine and are said to be a carrier. However, if you have two copies of the gene, you will fail to process a chemical found in most foods (phenylalanine). The result is that it will build to toxic levels that will lead to severe intellectual dysfunction. The mechanism is clear, and the genetic contribution is clear, so you would think that the heritability coefficient should be 1.00 (100 percent of the variability due to genes). But the heritability coefficient is much lower because we understand the disorder and can manipulate the environment with diet to prevent mental retardation. So in today's world, whether you show intellectual dysfunction from this cause depends in part on the genetic disease but also whether the disease is detected and whether the diet is adjusted appropriately. In developed countries, babies are tested for PKU routinely at or near birth, so the role of genes (and thus the heritability coefficient) is reduced. In third world countries, such testing and diets are less available, and thus most of the variability is the result of the genes.

The take-home message is clear. Genes clearly affect many of our skills, but genes always interact with the environment. It may help to think of genes as if they are light switches. Unless those switches are turned on by something in the environment, they have no impact. You may have genetically influenced musical talent, but if you never are exposed to music, you will not develop that talent. If you are exposed to music but you are unwilling to practice hard, you will likely be good at music but perhaps never good enough to be a superstar. In fact, there is overwhelming evidence that intense practice is necessary for success in almost every complex field, no matter how gifted a person may be (Ericsson, Krampe, & Tesch-Römer, 1993).

The Risks of a Fixed Mindset

It should be clear by now that intelligence is not a simple concept. Some elements of it are indeed fixed, but other elements are malleable. It is both fixed and changeable, or at least potentially changeable. So what difference does it make in how we look at a concept like intelligence?

How we look at intelligence influences our willingness to challenge ourselves to learn more. If you have a fixed mindset for intelligence, you believe that your level of intelligence is not changed by your effort to learn more. That decreases your motivation for learning. That is bad enough, but it is not the worst feature of a fixed mindset. With a fixed mindset, trying something difficult is an aversive experience. If you do something difficult, you are likely to fail and fail repeatedly until, after considerable effort, you finally learn how to succeed at this difficult task. In a fixed mindset, failing at something is proof that you do not have what it takes. In other words, you are not as smart as you thought you were. Such failures are a terrible blow to your ego, so you avoid challenging things, and as a result, you never really extend your abilities through diligent effort.

In a fixed mindset, failure is proof that you do not have the "right stuff." In contrast, a growth mindset suggests that failure is routine for anyone who wants to improve. Of course you will fail. What you are struggling to learn is new, and it will take time to master. But in a growth mindset, you believe that you can learn it if you have the time and energy to keep working on this new task. Now failure becomes a sign that you are on the right path, not a sign that you will never be able to succeed.

The Advantages of a Growth Mindset

A growth mindset promotes new learning because it both (1) defines ability as what you have learned and (2) avoids deflating your ego when your initial efforts to learn something new are insufficient to succeed. Frankly, there are few things in life that people get right the first time. Watch infants as they experiment with arm and leg movement until they can propel themselves forward in the desired direction. Clearly, at that age, children have a growth mindset. Most children still have that growth mindset when they are learning to ride a bike, play a new video game, or master a new sport. They do not expect to do it perfectly the first time. However, somewhere along the line, many people start to think differently about themselves and their place in the world. They learn about concepts like intelligence, and that knowledge changes their willingness to take new risks to learn difficult material. Unfortunately, fixed mindsets can be contagious because so many people use the language of a fixed mindset. If we are told we are smart, it becomes increasingly difficult to take on challenges that may suggest otherwise.

It is tempting to view this change in attitude as a moral failure. However, I do not believe that it is a character flaw. Our ego, or sense of ourselves, is fragile. The aversiveness that people feel when they fail is real, and it provides considerable motivation to work hard to succeed to avoid the sting of failure. But like many things in life, this is a delicate balance. We ideally need enough of this fear of failure to drive us to succeed, but if we have too much, we are driven to avoid taking chances on failing. The best way to avoid failure is to never take a chance. Unfortunately, this approach avoids failure at the cost of guaranteeing that you will never succeed.

Contributing in part to the fixed mindset may be the emphasis in schools on testing. Because of the importance placed on these tests, teachers are encouraged to "teach to the test." The implicit message is that these tests define ability, and one never wants to do badly on them for fear that he or she will forever be labeled inferior.

A growth mindset buffers our ego from the failure experiences that are all but guaranteed if we try new things. Failure is still frustrating, but a growth mindset reframes the experience as the price of getting better. This reframing of the inevitable failures of life can be the difference between losing hope and developing depression or redoubling your efforts and eventually succeeding.

This process is best illustrated with a psychological phenomenon called *learned helplessness* (Peterson & Seligman, 1984). This phenomenon was first recognized in animals and then later studied in human beings. When you place an animal in a situation that is aversive and inescapable, the animal typically stops trying to escape. We may conceptualize the animal's response as saving its energy for a time when it has control over the environment and escape is possible. The most interesting finding of this study is what happens a day or two later. If that same animal is placed in an aversive situation from which escape is easy and obvious, the animal makes no effort to escape. In comparison, animals not previously exposed to the inescapable aversive situation easily escape. Seligman, the experimental psychologist who discovered this phenomenon, argued that the animals had learned to be helpless.

Seligman was intrigued by this finding and even more intrigued that the dogs in his study showed many of the same characteristics that we find in depressed human beings. So, he retrained as a clinical psychologist and began to study this learned helplessness in human beings. Not surprisingly, the situation is more complicated with human beings. Some individuals did indeed show this learned helplessness phenomenon and signs of depression when faced with inescapable aversive situations. (Note, for ethical reasons, one cannot create a situation that leads to enough learned helplessness that the person is clinically depressed. However, life naturally creates such situations, and observing how people respond to them can give us real insights into their effects.)

People are constantly assessing their situation and responding to both the situation and their assessment of the situation. Some people who experience aversive situations show learned helplessness, but some clearly do not. Seligman and his colleagues discovered that the factor that predicted who would respond with helplessness was the attributions that the person made for their situation. *Attributions* are decisions about the likely reason for outcomes, both positive and negative. For example, if one fails an exam, one may assume (i.e., make an attribution) that the reason was that the exam was unreasonably difficult (an external attribution) or that one did not study hard enough (an internal attribution).

Seligman found that three dimensions of attributions were important in setting people up for depression when faced with aversive situations: internal/external, stable/unstable, and global/specific. Using the example of doing poorly on an exam, an internal attribution may be that you were not smart enough, and an external attribution may be that the exam was unfair. Blaming your poor performance on not being smart would also be a stable attribution if you consider intelligence a stable trait, whereas blaming your poor performance on being ill or not having time to study would be an unstable attribution. Telling yourself that you cannot do anything right is a global attribution, whereas telling yourself that this is a subject that is not one of your strengths is a specific attribution. People who make internal, stable, and global attributions for everyday failures in life tend to be at higher risk for developing depression. Think about that. You fail at something, and you interpret that failure to mean that (1) you do not have what it takes to succeed, (2) you have never had what it takes to succeed, and (3) you are a failure at everything you do. That certainly is a recipe for depression.

Let me emphasize one more thing: failure is universal. Everyone fails at one time or another. As I mentioned earlier, the people that we call winners are the ones who have learned to come back from losses. In fact, winners are the people who redouble their efforts in the face of defeat to avoid future losses. That is why the adoption of a growth mindset is so valuable to our emotional well-being as well as our long-term performance. When we label our failures as the necessary step toward being more successful, we avoid the destructive attributions that can lead us to give up and withdraw into a depressive state.

I want to make one more comment about attributions. We all know people who never take responsibility for any failure. For them, it is always someone else's fault or something outside of their control. These people can be obnoxious, and in general, they are not terribly successful in life. People are successful when they learn from their mistakes, and to learn from your mistakes, you must accept responsibility for them. Those who always blame others for their failures may be able to avoid depression, but unless their goal is to be a happy failure, that is not much of a consolation prize. So, your goal should not be to avoid internal attributions for the sake of your mental health. Your goal should be to reinterpret those internal attributions to protect your mental health while at the same time providing encouragement to improve your skills so that you can eventually succeed. That is what a growth mindset does. It reinterprets your internal attributions as the first step in redoubling your efforts to improve. Doing that is hard work, and you should praise yourself for having the courage to do that hard work.

Promoting a Growth Mindset

On paper, a growth mindset is ideal. How could anyone not want to develop that attitude? Instead of just resting on your reputational laurels, you strive to improve, you learn new things, and you stretch yourself, and in the process, you become the best person that you can be. When you say it that way, it is hard to resist. The reality is often more distressing than it sounds. People hate to fail, and the growth mindset represents deliberate failure, or at least a high probability of failure. In a growth mindset, you do not focus on what you do well; there is little to be gained there. Instead, you focus on those things you do not do well. In fact, you focus on those things that are your greatest weaknesses because you need to build those areas into new strengths. And once you get good at something, you refocus on other things that you do badly. It takes incredible emotional strength to maintain an attitude like that, and few people naturally have such strength.

There are three potential strategies that can promote a growth mindset. They are all well-known psychological principles. I will use their psychological names and explain each in turn. They are

18

cognitive behavioral therapy, social support, and *progress monitoring.*

Cognitive Behavioral Therapy

Cognitive behavioral therapy has a long history in clinical psychology (Leahy & Martell, 2021). As the name implies, it is a combination of two approaches: the behavioral approach, which focuses on behavior and its consequence, and the cognitive approach, which focuses on how we perceive and think about things and how those thoughts affect our emotional reactions and consequent behavior.

The core of behavior theory is deceptively simple. It is called the *law of effect* (Leahy & Martell, 2021). This law states that the likelihood of future behavior is influenced by the consequences of similar behavior in the past. So if you thank someone for helping you out, which is a positive consequence for their behavior, they are more likely to help you out in the future. If, on the other hand, you criticize their efforts to help you, which is a negative consequence for their behavior, they are less likely to help you out in the future. In common language, behavior that gets rewarded tends to be repeated; behavior that get punished tends not to be repeated.

As you think about the example above, you probably instinctively imagined talking to yourself when faced with such a situation. If your efforts to help someone in the past have been consistently rewarded, you are probably saying that you would be happy to help them in the future because they are so appreciative. If, on the other hand, you have been punished for trying to help, you likely are saying to yourself that there is no use trying because they do not appreciate your help and tend to be nasty instead of appreciative. Those are *cognitions*, which is a fancy word for *thoughts*. The cognitive model recognizes that our feelings and behavior are heavily influenced by our cognitions.

Our cognitions can sometimes override our instinctive response to the consequences of our behavior. If you offer words of support to a friend and that friend snaps at you in anger, your natural response is to be less likely to offer support in the future.

But you may think that your friend's behavior is out of character and that there may be something else happening. If you learn later that your friend was just turned down for a promotion, you may ignore his outburst because you believe it had nothing to do with you and more to do with the loss of the promotion. If your friend later apologizes for his outburst and explains that he was not angry with you but rather was upset by his boss not appreciating his work, that new information confirms your belief and likely will nullify the natural tendency of not wanting to be supportive in the future. Of course, this reinterpretation works in this situation because the person who lashed out is a friend and you are likely to keep an open mind and be in close enough contact that the additional information about the situation comes out. Imagine how things would turn out if we are talking about a single encounter with someone we will never see again.

People are thinking all the time about what is happening to them and why. Our thoughts often give us insights into complex situations and, therefore, modify our behavior to make it more effective. For example, if we had planned on asking for a raise and our boss comes in obviously angry because of things that happened at home, we may recognize that bosses in a bad mood are less likely to think kindly of our request for a raise. Therefore, we wait a day or two before we ask, perhaps after we have had a chance to show how valuable we are to the company.

Although I am a big believer that our ability to think is an incredible gift, as a clinical psychologist, I know that sometimes our thoughts can be our own worst enemy. It is common for people to overreact to things, interpreting the situation incorrectly. For example, many people overreact to mistakes, beating themselves up for making those mistakes. The thoughts that often go along with those emotional reactions include things like, "I have to be perfect," or, "No one will respect me if I am not perfect." When you say such things out loud, it is easy to see that the thoughts are unreasonable and even irrational, but often the thoughts are outside of our awareness. Nevertheless, they still shape how we feel, but because we never clearly articulate them, we have no chance to challenge them.

So how do these behavioral and cognitive strategies influence our mindsets? If we try to do something and we fail, that is an aversive state. It punishes us for doing, or trying to do, that activity. We all know that we prefer to do things that we do well and tend to avoid things that we do not do well. Therefore, we tend to behave as if we have a fixed mindset, avoiding challenging tasks that we are unlikely to succeed at initially.

This is a perfect example of behavioral principles reinforcing a fixed mindset. But remember that our cognitions also affect our responses. If we allow ourselves to interpret each failure as evidence that we are incompetent, then we have cranked up the aversiveness to a higher level. If we have a fixed mindset, that is exactly the interpretation we would make. In fact, under the assumption of a fixed mindset, such interpretations are entirely logical. A fixed mindset says that we are either good or not. If we are good, we will be consistently successful. If we are not good, we will not be successful. So our failures represent evidence that we are not good and therefore can expect to fail consistently. Again, when we spell it out like that, we can see the flaws in our argument, but we often are unaware of the logical flow of our thoughts. We just experience the emotional impact that these thoughts produce. However, we can learn to identify these thoughts and challenge them when they are negatively affecting our emotional stability.

A growth mindset requires constant cognitive interventions because those interventions must override the natural behavioral responses to failure. Failure is aversive. I have never met someone who liked failure. Even masochists, who seem to crave pain, try to avoid failure. But if you reframe the failure cognitively, you can reframe your emotional response to the failure. Instead of focusing on your failure, you focus on the issue of how to succeed on the next trial. Instead of focusing on failure, you complement yourself for being willing and able to extend your abilities. Finally, instead of comparing yourself to those who can do what you just failed at, compare yourself to those who do not have the courage to risk failure to improve. Your failure can thus be transformed from a humiliation to a sign of courage and a hopeful signpost on your way to even greater success.

Social Support

By nature, we are social creatures, and social support is critical to our optimal functioning. It plays a particularly important role in a growth mindset because a growth mindset encourages us to take on challenges that we are not yet able to complete. That means that we will be faced with multiple failures, which can be demoralizing. But being around other people who also have growth mindsets means that we can share each other's distress and encourage and reward the efforts to continue to grow.

Parents often are concerned about their children's friends. The reason is simple. The people around us influence us in both positive and negative ways. If your friends like to push boundaries and thus often get into trouble, chances are you will get into trouble with them. If they love to play sports, chances are you will be playing sports with them. If they work hard to succeed, likely you will share those same goals. You likely selected your friends because they share your goals, and thus you support each other in the efforts to achieve those goals. We all need a little nudge to keep pushing toward our goals, and when we stumble, we need a hand to get back up and try again.

Coaches often emphasize a growth mindset. To improve the team, they challenge each team member to develop new skills and to work on their weaknesses until those weaknesses become strengths. This aspect of the growth mindset has been a part of sports long before the name *growth mindset* was coined by Carol Dweck. Teams have an advantage in this growth-directed effort because they automatically provide social support. Every member of the team wants to succeed, and every member of the team understands that success rests on both their effort and the effort of all the other team members. A good coach models social support by praising efforts even when players fall short. This encourages players to keep working, and when they succeed, the reward is enormous.

In time, team members provide the critical support for other team members to work to improve. This support may be little more than saying that you notice how hard a team member is working to improve and perhaps adding that you believe in them. A team member may also praise teammates for any improvement over time. These supportive elements bridge the gap between the initial frustrating failure and the eventual joy of succeeding. We love to be praised for success, but success is its own reward. What we need most from teammates, friends, coaches, teachers, and parents is support through the frustrations in the struggle to succeed.

Traditionally, academic institutions have not been thought of as teams. That is unfortunate. First, teams naturally provide the support that team members need. That support is harder to get if you function as an individual with no concept of a team. There are other reasons to structure education as a team effort. The best way to learn material, as you will learn in the next chapter, is to teach that material to other people. Students working together often produce more learning in both the stronger and the weaker students.

The best way to get social support is to be around people who share your values. In a university setting, there are often formal and informal organizations that attract people with similar values. For example, a university's honor program will include strong students who are highly motivated to succeed. Being actively involved in such programs and taking courses with honors students is a natural way to get support for a growth mindset. Many academic departments have clubs, organizations, or honors societies that bring together students committed to the academic discipline and to success in that discipline.

There are often university-wide programs that attract like-minded and committed students. These may include the school newspaper, service organizations, or organizations focused on activities. College athletics certainly qualify, but few students possess the skills to join college teams. However, most schools have a variety of intramural athletic groups in which students compete against fellow students at the university. Getting involved in any of these organizations is valuable and can provide the emotional support needed to challenge yourself continually to get better.

Progress Monitoring

One of the most effective ways of providing personal support and maximizing your efforts to improve is to monitor your progress. Monitoring your progress accomplishes two goals. One, it tells you whether your efforts are leading to improved performance. If the efforts are not leading to improvement, perhaps you need to rethink your strategy for improvement. Two, monitoring progress is enormously rewarding when you can see evidence that you are getting better.

Such records are routinely kept by sports teams, and good coaches use those statistical records to focus their work with individual team members. Such records are also a routine part of any college course, and some teachers will actively use those records to help coach students. However, the classroom is typically conceptualized differently than a sports team, and teachers usually view their task as imparting wisdom and answering questions rather than coaching students. That is a shame because a coaching attitude could go a long way in a classroom. However, just because the professor does not want to be a coach does not mean that you cannot coach yourself by trying different strategies and monitoring their effectiveness. You may, for example, change the way you study a subject and observe how well you do on the course exams or assignments.

Progress monitoring does not have to rely on course grades, which at best are crude indicators of progress. For example, it is a good idea to keep the papers you write for classes and periodically review them. If you have been working to improve your writing skills, such a review can be incredibly rewarding. We rarely see the progress we are making on a skill like writing until we compare our current work against papers that we wrote a year or two earlier. Moreover, reviewing such papers not only allows us to see our improvement in writing, but also our improvement in our conceptual and organizational skills.

If you combine social support and progress monitoring, you may take courses with friends who share your goals. You can study together, challenging each other to do better and supporting the efforts of one another. This kind of experience will improve all-around performance for everyone in the group.

Chapter Summary

The key to ultimate success is constant growth and development. However, growth requires taking risks by attempting things that you know you do not (yet) do well. That means you will fail until you master the new task, and most people hate failing. The growth mindset provides both a rationale and a mechanism to manage the frustration as you strive to master new material.

The growth mindset encourages taking risks by committing to learning things that you currently do not do well. Although it can be frustrating during such efforts, the payback is an advance in your skills and experience, which will dramatically improve your chances of career success. You can ease the frustrations using several psychological techniques, including cognitive behavioral therapy, social support, and progress monitoring.

Chapter 3
Learning How to Learn

I f you are reading this book, you may be telling yourself that you do not need this chapter. Individuals who read this book are almost always good students who are highly motivated to succeed in school and beyond. You clearly know how to study. In fact, I suspect some readers are skipping this chapter because it seems so irrelevant. If you are tempted to skip this chapter, give me a couple of pages to convince you that, despite all your hard work in studying, you can learn how to study more effectively. When you study more effectively, you can successfully compete against people who are just as smart and just as disciplined as you because you will be able to learn better and with less effort.

Before you get too excited, I am not promising that learning will be easy. Learning is difficult, and some learning is very difficult. That is why learning is such a valuable skill and marketable asset. You will discover in this chapter that there are better ways to learn than most people use. Moreover, you will discover that most people focus on inputting information in their learning when the real goal should be to put it in so that you can get it out. You have likely taken a test in which you knew that you knew the answer, but you could not remember it during the test. You want to avoid that frustration.

Much of the material in this chapter comes from a twenty-minute bonus lecture that I typically give shortly after the first exam in my classes. The purpose of the lecture is to inform students of better ways to study the material and therefore better ways to get a good grade. Frankly, students are more interested in getting a good grade than I am, but they usually take this lecture to heart because it works. I am more interested in their learning, and I am especially interested in them learning how to learn more effectively. I am amazed every semester at how many students single out this short topic as one of the most valuable parts of the entire class.

What Does It Take to Learn?

The best way to illustrate the difference between studying and learning is with an example that almost every student has experienced. You sit down one evening to catch up on some studying and open a text. You spend three hours reading two chapters; you read every single word; you are reading carefully and not skimming. Yet, at the end of the evening, you realize you do not remember a single thing that you read. What a waste of effort!

How could such a thing happen? It happens more often than you realize, or maybe you do realize it because it has happened to you several times. At this stage in your life, reading is so easy for you that you can do it without thinking. Unfortunately, you cannot learn without thinking. Reading and learning are very different processes. Because reading is often part of learning, we assume that is how learning is done, but that assumption is dead wrong. Learning is much harder than experiencing something. It takes significant effort to learn. It is not something we do well when we are tired. It almost always requires repeated exposure, and typically the exposure needs to be over days. A simple example is someone giving you their phone number that you quickly dial. Unless you are trying to remember that phone number, you will forget it within seconds after dialing it. Fortunately, modern cell phones will remember the numbers that you dialed, but that is a recent advance. Not remembering things like phone numbers is not a limitation of our brain and memory; it is just how our memory works. In this chapter, I will give a brief overview of how memory works and what you can do to enhance it. I will finish the chapter by giving you methods that will improve how much you learn for a given amount of effort.

Learning as Associations

I have always argued that you do not have to be religious to look at the magnificent capabilities of humans and see them as miraculous.

Virtually all our capabilities reside in the three pounds of matter that make up our brain. Although we do not understand everything there is to know about our brain, our understanding of the brain has expanded dramatically in the last fifty years (see Gazzaniga & Mangun, 2014).

Most people think of the human brain as a computer, but that is not a good model of how the brain works. Granted, both our brain and the computer can solve problems, and both have the potential of expanding their capabilities (through software and hardware upgrades in the computer and learning in human beings). But those are surface features. Below the surface, our brain and traditional computers have almost nothing in common. Unlike computers, our brains do not allow us to add memory or computing power. Unlike computers, our brains are gradually dying, one brain cell (neuron) at a time. However, those brain cells add up. It is estimated that we lose fifty thousand individual neurons each day on average, although some scientists question the exact number. That sounds like a massive loss of brain functioning, but we start with somewhere between ten billion and one hundred billion neurons. The amazing thing is that the wiring of the brain compensates for these neuronal losses, and we typically do not see serious disruption in our cognitive functioning from neuronal loss until late in life (Williamson & Allman, 2011).

The wiring of the brain also allows the brain to organize the information as it comes in. It accomplishes this organization because the brain is so heavily interconnected (McClelland, 2011). On average, each nerve cell or neuron is connected to approximately one thousand other neurons. Information is stored by the pattern of connections. One aspect of this organizational system is that concepts that overlap tend to be stored in a way that the conceptual overlap, or association, is recorded. That is why a particular memory will often lead us to recover related memories. A simple example of that is probably something you have experienced. You walk into a room to get something, and you cannot remember what you wanted to get. Typically, if you walk back into the room in which you first had that thought, the room will trigger a recall of your original desire. Your original thought was associated with the place in which you originally had that thought, and if you just had that thought a few seconds earlier, the connection is still strong enough that walking back into the same room is enough to trigger the thought a second time. There has been extensive study of this process in psychology and neuroscience under the name of *connectionist models* or *parallel distributed processing* (PDP). This topic is too complex to cover here, but the interested reader can learn more about it in McClelland and Rumelhart (1988).

So, why talk about how the brain is wired when all you really want to know is how to put the material that you need to learn into your brain? After all, you do not need to know how an internal combustion engine works to drive a car. Well, you do not need to know how the brain is wired either, but it helps to know how the brain works if you want to maximize your learning.

The brain is capable of amazing things, but what it does best is learn associations. Associations are links between ideas. The most common association to the word *black* is *white*, to the word *up* is *down*, and to the word *male* is *female*. These associations are the opposite of one another. Other associations are *driving* and *car*, *throwing* and *ball*, and *sleeping* and *bed*. These associations are between an action and an object. But think about these associations for a minute. The word *car* comes to mind when you think of *driving*, but what comes to mind when you think about the word *car*? It probably is not *driving*, but rather something like *truck* or *road*. These are examples of associations that are more directional. When you think of driving, you think of what you are likely to be driving (i.e., a *car*) because very few people drive trucks, buses, or tanks. To illustrate this directionality, recite the alphabet (*A* through *Z*). Now recite it backward. Normally, every letter triggers the letter that follows it in our learning (*A* then *B*; *P* then *Q*), but it does not trigger the letter that precedes it (*B* then *A*; *Q* then *P*).

Not being able to recite the alphabet backward may seem irrelevant, but it is not. If you read that Thomas Jefferson designed and built his home near Charlottesville, Virginia, you will find it much easier to answer the question, "Where did Thomas Jefferson build his home?" than the question, "Which president lived near

Charlottesville, Virginia?" On the surface, that seems crazy. But just like it is easier to say that the letter *I* follows *H* than to say that the letter *G* precedes *H*, when we learn a fact in one direction, it is always easier to recall that fact in the direction that we learned it.

If you want to recall relevant information regardless of your starting point or the direction of the question, you need to learn the information from multiple points of view. If you just read a textbook chapter, you are likely to get the information presented in one specific direction only. Let's use an example. Suppose that you read that John Adams was the second president of the United States. You may be surprised to learn that how a question is asked will influence how likely you are to recall that information. The apparently identical questions of "Who is John Adams?" and "Who was the second president of the United States?" may differ on the likelihood of being answered correctly. That effect is most pronounced after a brief reading of a chapter. However, it almost completely disappears if you process the information more deeply.

What do I mean by processing the information more deeply? Although it is difficult to define precisely, it involves thinking about the meaning of what you read rather than the literal words you read. You do that routinely in everyday life but often fail to do it when you read your textbook. An example will illustrate this process. A friend tells you, "Robert just fired Ellie." These are people that you both know well. An hour later, you tell one of Ellie's friends, "Ellie just got fired." You are passing on information, a process that you do several times a day with your friends and colleagues, but you are doing more than that. You are passing on not what you were told, but the deeper meaning of what you were told. You understood that an actor (Robert) performed an action (firing) on an object (Ellie). You used entirely different words to describe what you learned, leaving out information that was probably not as important to Ellie's friend (specifically, who did the firing) but including more relevant information (i.e., the action that affected Ellie: being fired).

When we engage in conversation, we try to understand what is being said and how it affects us and the others in the conversation. If there is ambiguity, we may ask for clarification. For example, if

Ellie's friend has more than one friend named Ellie, she may ask for clarification on which Ellie we are talking about. But when we are reading, especially if we are reading on autopilot, we do not process deeply. Our understanding is much closer to the specific words rather than the deep meaning of those words. In the next section, we will talk about how you need to read your textbook to process the deeper meaning of the words in the text and to organize that information so it is readily recalled no matter how someone asks the question.

We store a lot of information in our brain, but that information may be buried in such a way that recalling it when asked a direct question is difficult. Let's return to the earlier example of Thomas Jefferson's hometown. Often, we do not remember the answer to a question, but we remember something about the question that will link us to associated information, which is information that may or may not be relevant for our task. For example, if we are asked which president lived in Charlottesville, Virginia, we may have little clue, but we may search for the answer by looking for things we know about Charlottesville and Virginia. We may remember, for example, that many of our forefathers were from Virginia, so it is likely that we are talking about one of the first few presidents. We may also remember that Charlottesville is the home of the University of Virginia because the basketball team from the university that we attended played an important game there. Perhaps, by chance, we remember seeing a statue of Thomas Jefferson when we were on campus to see the game. We recognized the statue because we saw pictures of Jefferson in our high school history book, where we learned that Jefferson was a forefather and a president. We may infer that his statue on the campus may suggest that he lived in the area. In other words, one memory leads to other memories, which leads to still other memories, often to the point that we "discover" in our mind the answer to the question. Each memory is associated with those other memories, which is how a memory leads us to other memories.

If you have ever played a trivia game with partners, such as Trivial Pursuit, you can often see this process at work. No one on the team knows the answer, but one or two members may know something about the topic. Putting what they know out there often triggers memories in other team members, and those memories may trigger other memories until eventually the team that seemed not to know the answer will find the answer. It appears magical, but it is just how the brain works.

When we talk about strategies for learning, we will use this principle extensively. The key is, if you want to be able to reliably find the information you need in your brain when you need it, you need to encode it in such a manner that the question will tend to lead you to the answer. Knowing something by itself is useless unless you can recall it when you need it. Recalling it a minute after you read it does not help on the test, and it will not help on most tasks once you graduate.

What Needs to Be Learned?

The amount you can learn is unlimited; the amount of time you have available to learn is not. The result is that a smart learner will not waste time learning things that can easily be looked up. The same is true for skills. I have always been good at math, and when I was in high school, I could flawlessly multiply three- and four-digit numbers against one another in my head. That was handy in the store I worked at when we took our annual inventory. I could multiply, for example, 117 units times $17.85 and come up with $2,088.45. I was at least as accurate as a calculator, which at the time was prohibitively expensive. My boss loved me. Today, I use a calculator to balance my checkbook. Why? Because it is easy. Today, I would not even need to punch in the numbers to solve the inventory question above. I can say, "Hey Siri, how much is 117 times 17.85?" and my phone will give me the answer.

People built monuments with simple hand tools and muscles. Massive canal systems, the pyramids, and the roads and viaducts going back to the Roman Empire were built with muscle power primarily. We build the same things today with a fraction of the effort and in a fraction of the time by using equipment much more powerful than our muscles. It only makes sense that the introduction of thinking machines, such as computers, would have the same impact on intellectual tasks.

So what things are worth learning? Rather than learning the mechanics of computing statistics by hand, we need to learn how to interpret those statistics. For example, one should be suspicious of a mean score of 17.44 if the scores were all between 3 and 16. The mean should be roughly in the middle of the scores and certainly not outside of the range of the scores. In general, computers do not think; they compute. It is likely that there is an error in data entry if your mean is impossible given the data. Even in artificial intelligence, computers do the computation, but it is the software that checks to make sure the computations are reasonable.

As computers and calculators take over computational tasks, the focus is on understanding the output and making optimal decisions based on that output. My parlor trick of being able to multiply large numbers against one another has little value today. The ability to interpret the output from massive computer systems that crunch billions of numbers with large data sets can be the difference between a company succeeding and failing. It is the era of big data, and the people who understand how to use big data will have the jobs of the future.

Some skills will always be critical. The strength of human beings is our ability to work cooperatively with other people. Granted, human beings tend to be good at solving problems, but when we work together with other human beings, we solve bigger problems and come up with better solutions. So communication will never go out of favor. Writing so our intentions are clear and precise will always be valuable. If you know how to do something but your writing is so sloppy that your employees cannot follow your instructions, you have failed. If your employees cannot understand language with sufficient clarity to follow clear instructions, they will have failed, but you will have failed for hiring them.

Communication involves both writing and oral communication. These skills share things in common, but because of the way that information is processed, we need to use different strategies. A sentence that is ambiguous is terrible whether you

33

wrote it or spoke it. However, written communication can be reread, whereas verbal communication is often heard only once. That is why students are often taught that when they are giving a speech, they should (1) tell the audience what they will say, (2) say it, and (3) tell them what they said. That does not mean that you say the same thing three times, but rather that you need to outline before and summarize after for the listener. Moreover, unless you are speaking to hundreds or thousands of people, it would be advisable to ask if they understood what you said and then verify that they understood it correctly by asking them to repeat back the instructions. Your communications need not be as awe-inspiring as Martin Luther King Jr.'s "I Have a Dream" speech. If you can do that, you likely have a great future, because being inspiring is a truly valuable skill. But for most people, communicating clearly and precisely gets the job done. The next chapter focuses on the critical skill of communicating effectively.

What other skills are important to learn? I include two skills in this category. The first is to be able to think critically about a problem. Critical thinking is an unfortunate choice of words to describe the systematic evaluation of the logic of arguments and the data available to support or refute those arguments. Many students incorrectly believe that critical thinkers are people who criticize every idea. True critical thinkers criticize weak ideas but readily accept strong ideas. Every educational program I know argues that its primary goal is to teach students to think critically, but the available research suggests that the educational system is by and large doing a poor job of this (Mirkin & Raulin, 2016; Wolf & Raulin, 2017).

The second issue is that one needs to learn "how to learn." Everything you learn in school will be outdated before you reach middle age, and some of it will be outdated in a matter of months. Long after you finish school, you will still need to keep learning. If you are not learning, you likely will be unable to compete in the fast-moving economy of today. And it does not matter what your occupation is. Every career is changing rapidly, and all the available evidence suggests that the pace of that rapid change is increasing. It is not uncommon today to have people retire, not because they no longer can do the job, but because they no longer have the drive to keep learning how to do the job better.

Strategies for Learning

How do we put these principles of how memory works and what is important to learn to good use? In this section, I will briefly describe strategies that will increase the efficiency of your studying.

Study Habits

The most important strategy to improve your learning is to develop a systematic and disciplined study program. If you fall behind and spend an entire day and night cramming for an exam, expect to do poorly. In contrast, if you study one hour a day every day for a week, you will learn more than twice as much as you would learn from studying seven hours the day before the exam. Same time spent, same effort, twice as much learning. To me, that is a no-brainer.

If you really want to shoot yourself in the foot, stay up all night studying for an exam the next day. Our brain functions optimally when we get sufficient rest, relaxation, activity, and nourishment. Being sleep deprived guarantees that your brain will not function well. Anything you might have learned overnight will be offset by your inability to kick your brain into high gear. To illustrate how strong this effect is, research shows that being sleep deprived can be more dangerous than being drunk when it comes to driving safely (Philip et al., 2002). Hopefully, you will never consider driving if you consume too much alcohol. But sleep deprivation can have an even more powerful effect than alcohol on your ability to drive safely.

Unless you have a photographic memory, which is rare and surprisingly of little use, you will learn little on your first exposure. Instead, it takes repeated exposures for a memory to become solid and easily accessed. An implication is that reading the material once and only once is a recipe for poor academic performance. In the next section, we will talk about the difference between having a memory and being able to recall it when needed. Moreover, there is good evidence that suggests that one of the functions of sleep is that it consolidates important memories while we sleep (Maquet, 2001). That is probably the main reason why spreading out your studying over several days is more effective than doing all your studying in a single day. Usually, when students do all their studying in a single day, it is because they only have one day left and they have no choice but to cram (i.e., try to shove as much into their brain as they can in a short time).

Most experiences are not worth remembering. We retain the memory for a short period just in case it proves to be useful, but we never put it in more permanent storage accessible to us later. For example, you probably do not remember what you had for lunch on Tuesday of last week, but who cares? If you want to remember something, you generally must try to remember it. Cognitive psychologists have a name for this process: elaborative rehearsal. In *elaborative rehearsal*, we consciously try to remember something, and we enhance our ability to remember that thing by relating it to other things of interest. For example, we may remember that we had a hamburger for lunch on Tuesday because we stopped by McDonald's with a friend. If something is important to remember, we will likely use elaborative rehearsal over several days. Each elaborative rehearsal increases the strength of the memory and therefore makes it more likely that we can recover the memory later.

The most valuable thing you can do to improve how much you learn from your study sessions is to spread your studying over several days. Cognitive psychologists call this *spaced practice*, as opposed to *massed practice*, which is what you do when you cram for an exam.

You can take this basic study strategy and enhance it even more by making sure that your study sessions overlap. Start studying each day by briefly reviewing what you learned in the previous day. This highlights the most important points you want to remember and makes it more likely that the strength of those memories will increase. Then study the new material. If you want to make this principle even more effective, end the session by previewing what you intend to study the next day. If you always review the material from the previous day and preview the material for the next day, you will have at least three instances in which the material is processed and thus the memory strengthened.

Building Multiple Associations

We talked about how the brain is naturally wired to organize associations, which represent connections between ideas. We naturally see and organize such associations, but if we take an active role in our learning to identify and formally recognize associations between concepts, we will accomplish two goals. One, we will dramatically increase the likelihood that we will be able to recall critical information regardless of how the instructor asks us about that information. Two, we will automatically prioritize our studying on the most important material. Each related idea to a concept is an important association. Having many associations demonstrates the importance of a concept, and the focus on each of these relevant associations provides the repeated exposure to the material that makes spaced practice so effective.

You cannot build these kinds of relevant associations between ideas by just reading the textbook. The kind of high-quality studying that leads to real learning requires energy, focus, and serious concentration. Instead of just reading the material, you need to focus on processing it. But a simple process of adjusting your reading approach will dramatically improve the efficiency of your initial reading. Start by stopping your reading at the end of each paragraph and ask yourself what you just read. Then ask yourself how it relates to other things you also read in the text and other things you know from other sources. Finally, generate real-life examples of the concept or the situations in which that concept would be relevant. These last two approaches are particularly valuable. Things you already know typically have a rich associational network, so linking your new concepts to them links them to your already present and usually strong associational network. Developing your own examples requires high-level processing of information, so those examples and the ideas on which they are based tend to be remembered well.

These associational strategies require more time during the initial reading, but they are so much more effective that this additional time is cost-effective. There is another advantage to this strategy that I mentioned earlier; there is no way that the associational strategy for reading that I just outlined would ever allow you to spend two hours reading the material so casually that you do not remember anything.

This associational strategy should be continued after you have completed the initial reading of course materials. The worst mistake students make is to use a highlighter. Did your entire body stiffen at that last statement? How else do you study but to highlight the important material and then review the highlighted material when it comes time to study for the exam? The problem with highlighting is that it focuses on facts, and the facts are almost always out of context. Memorizing facts is almost as hard as memorizing phone numbers. Our brain is not built to do it well. To really learn the material, we should focus on how the facts fit together, which is what associational learning is all about.

If you have already highlighted your text, do not try to memorize what you highlighted. Instead, try to relate the material to other concepts from the course and your own knowledge. This strategy will not only strengthen the memory of those ideas in your brain but also will organize the information so it is readily recoverable from many different directions.

As you study more, go beyond the associations you recognize and try to create integrative stories that tie all the material together. There is a trick to help you with this next step. Do not think of yourself as a student; think of yourself as an instructor who is trying to get your presentation of the material organized for your class or tutoring session with another student. Have you ever noticed that your best teachers often seem to be telling stories? The stories make the class more interesting, but they also make the learning easier. Human beings have been telling stories to one another long before we had written language to write them down. The story format is so good at organizing information that a good story can be repeated over and over with remarkable fidelity.

Studying by making associations and then later constructing coherent stories is not only much more effective than trying to memorize the material, but it is also more enjoyable and a lot less drudgery. Don't believe me? Good! I want you to be skeptical. But give it a chance and try it yourself. I am betting you will happily drop your old ways of studying and replace them with what I suggest in this section.

Focus on Both Input and Output

Few students seem to understand that learning involves both input and output. All the focus seems to be on the input, with the assumption that output will take care of itself. Of course, if you never read the material or listen to a lecture, you will not have any input and therefore will not learn anything. In most courses, the input comes primarily from reading textbooks and listening to lectures. Output is the retrieval of information in response to specific questions or tasks. That is usually done through exams, papers, or discussions. You cannot learn without input, but the whole point of learning is to be able to access the material when necessary (i.e., output).

Traditionally, college courses have emphasized input and use exams and papers to assess output and learning. There is a recently developed model called the *flipped classroom*, which emphasizes output more (Keengwa, Onchwari, & Oigara, 2014). In the flipped classroom, the traditional lecture is either recorded and made available to students before class or eliminated. Instead, classroom time is focused on asking students questions, which range from traditional multiple-choice questions to complex questions that require students to integrate ideas. This approach works better in smaller classes in which the instructor can call on students to answer questions. The research shows that even when the student does not know the answer, the effort to try to recall the answer or figure it out will often help the student remember it in the future (Love, Hodge, Corritore, & Ernst, 2015). When done well, such a class can be interesting and effective in promoting learning, although many students are, at least initially, stressed out by the possibility that they will be called on to answer questions.

As textbooks increasingly go electronic, there is no need for the textbook to be a passive reading experience. Most electronic textbooks include questions that are integrated into the reading. These questions can be graded, and the grades automatically transferred to an electronic grade book. Such questions force students to think about the material as they read it, so it is impossible for them to read an entire chapter on autopilot and not learn a single thing. Each time students think about a question, they process the information they just read. Such textbooks can also include material presented in alternative ways, such as film clips or explaining ideas visually for the reader. These alternative approaches often enhance the learning of students.

You can take this principle a step further by looking at the material from the standpoint of what the instructor is most likely to ask about on the exam. This is an active exercise that most students find inherently rewarding. Hopefully, the instructor will be most likely to ask about the important issues, so this exercise will focus you on those issues. It also engages you in an analysis process of reading the intentions and goals of another person (i.e., your professor). Being able to carefully observe and interpret the actions of others is an invaluable skill that is rarely covered in traditional educational settings but that will serve people well in the real world.

A flipped classroom or an electronic textbook with embedded questions facilitates learning because it requires students to actively process what they read. If students have learned the information well, they will easily answer the questions. If students have only vaguely learned the material, they will struggle to find the answer and, in the process of struggling to find it, will organize the information more effectively. The next time the student faces the same question or similar question, he or she is more likely to either recall or figure out the answer.

The effectiveness of a flipped classroom is impressive compared to a traditional lecture format (Keengwa et al., 2014). Electronic textbooks include embedded questions because the textbook is more effective with such questions (activelylearn.com). But, as a student, you can take a traditional class with a traditional textbook and lecture format and build these elements into your study process, which will focus you on both the input and the output. This could start with something as simple as stopping at the end of each paragraph and asking yourself what you read.

You can enhance your learning in other ways that will improve your ability to recall the information when needed. As I mentioned earlier, one of the most common but least effective strategies is to highlight the material as you read. Students typically review the highlighted material while studying for an exam. You already learned that this tends not to be effective because it focuses on unrelated facts rather than the relationships (i.e., associations) among those facts. But it is also generally ineffective because it only focuses on input. You can focus your reading more on output by constantly asking yourself questions beyond what you just read in the previous paragraph.

The way you take notes in class and while studying also makes a difference. The process of writing down the material increases the likelihood that we will remember the material. It is another way of providing input. There is research that suggests that, for most people, handwriting the notes is more effective than typing the notes. The reason for this finding is unclear, but people have speculated that we are so used to handwriting notes that we can focus more on the content when recording notes that way compared to typing. This is a line of research that may deserve more study. When the work was first done, most of the subjects were not raised with constant access to computers. It may well be that the experience of typing ideas rather than writing them down would change how effectively one learns from typing notes. This is an example of an important principle: our ideas about the best way of doing things are not written in stone. Things change, and smart people keep asking skeptical questions about the best way to do things.

College-level courses rarely focus on memorizing facts, which is typically the material that students highlight when reading. Instead, college courses focus on integrating ideas and showing how those ideas interact with one another. Asking yourself how the paragraph you just read relates to other things in the text begins that process of integrating ideas. Asking how what you just read is related to things you know from other courses promotes even more integration. Asking yourself to develop a realistic example takes the integration to an even higher level. Questions like these, which any student can learn to ask while reading and studying, not only make it easier to remember the material, but also build in the associative connections that allow you to find information that is not perfectly organized in your mind. We have all done that. We cannot remember someone's name, but we remember things about them, conversations we have had with them, other people that they know, and so on. That process of trying to recall as much as you can about the person often triggers the spontaneous recovery of the person's name. This will be the focus of the next section.

Finally, focusing on facts when you are learning will often prevent the kind of long-term retention of information that you are after. Facts are much more easily forgotten or misremembered than ideas or concepts. Ideas and concepts make good stories, and we are much better at remembering a good story than the contents of a dictionary.

Integrating Knowledge

The brain is often compared to a computer, but as we discussed earlier, it is not a good comparison. Computers are exceptionally good at storing information and finding it quickly because they move so quickly. Human beings find information quickly if, and only if, it is properly organized. For human beings, "properly organized" means having related ideas connected to one another. This produces a situation that seems counterintuitive. It is often easier to learn information by learning more information than you need rather than focusing on certain critical information. Focusing on certain critical information is a bit like having a telephone book. Telephone books have lots of unrelated information. Your phone can search your contacts in a second or two even if it is a long contact list. But as you learned, human memory organizes information as a series of associations. If we can recognize and recall a person quickly no matter what the situation, it is probably because we have stored enough information to provide almost every conceivable associational link to the person and the person's name.

We talked earlier about the last step in building an associational network of ideas from a course by seeking to create stories to remember those associations. There is an even higher level of organization that students should strive to achieve. That level is an integration that cuts across courses, fields, and perspectives.

Students typically mark their progress in college by how many courses or credits they have completed. That is fine, but it tends to make students think of those courses as individual units of study. A college education is not forty separate units (120 credits for a degree divided by 3 credits per course). The effectiveness of a college education is how well that set of units or courses produce a better understanding than the sum of those courses. The truly educated college student, who is the one most likely to get into advanced programs of study, is the one who integrates ideas from multiple courses to develop a higher level of understanding. Some advanced courses in a discipline will help you do that integration by reviewing earlier material you covered and then building on it in the course. Many fields of study require students to do a capstone project that requires such integration of ideas. But frankly, if you want to achieve that level of understanding, you will have to do most of the work on your own.

One way to enhance this extensive integration is to find another strong student with the same desire to reach another level of understanding. By working together on a regular basis to seek greater integration of ideas, you can make the task even more interesting and exciting. Moreover, invariably you will find that you periodically will need to explain your integration ideas. Nothing helps you learn better than trying to teach the material and concepts to someone else.

Finally, the world is integrating ideas to develop even better ideas all the time, and we can learn about those advances in the news. If your field is business, the best way to integrate the ideas you have learned in your courses is to keep up with what is happening in business. This approach also works for fields like education, science, and medicine and gives you the advantage of being prepared for your intended field by staying informed of its advances.

Periodically Review to Keep Information Fresh

We do not always know the mechanisms by which memories are formed and fade, but there is extensive research on the factors that influence this process. You have already learned that memories take time to form in a way that is accessible to you. Once a memory is formed, each time you access it, it becomes easier to access it in the future. Information that you use every day will usually be readily available to you. However, you have probably experienced one of those rare exceptions when, on a given day, you just could not retrieve memories that were normally always accessible.

There will always be important memories that we do not use every day. There are other memories that were once strong but have not been accessed for so long that recovering them on cue may be difficult. However, with just a little effort, we can refresh these memories and make them more readily available. This may be necessary when you take a course that is built on principles that you learned in a previous course, principles that you have not used for months or years. It may only take an hour or two to refresh your memory on these concepts. Many textbooks will take the time to have a review section of such concepts, but you cannot count on that.

Another situation involves materials you may have used years earlier but have not used recently. I teach psychology and therefore advise psychology students. Unlike other disciplines, psychology typically does not routinely include mathematical concepts. So when psychology students want to apply to graduate school, they will have to take the Graduate Record Exam (GRE). The GRE has a section on mathematics, which is not difficult if you have been using mathematics routinely. However, if your only exposure to mathematics was a single course taken your freshman year and your high school mathematics courses, you are likely to be rusty. For example, you may vaguely remember that there was something called a quadratic equation. You may even have a vague recollection of what that is. But the odds are good that you do not remember how to solve a quadratic equation systematically. However, just twenty hours of studying these basic math concepts will refresh your memory sufficiently that you can do reasonably well on the GRE. Most students in fields like psychology require that review. When I took the GREs, I had just become a psychology major but had previously been a chemistry major, with several courses in chemistry, physics, and mathematics. I did not need to review the mathematics because I had been using it regularly. If your major is physics, mathematics, or engineering, you likely will not need to review mathematics to do well on the GREs. However, you may need to review skills that are tested on other sections of the GREs that are not used every day in your major.

Chapter Summary

Students, even strong and hard-working college students, are often unaware of the best strategies to learn new material and remember it over time. This chapter covered strategies that can dramatically improve the quality of one's learning. These strategies are based on extensive research into how we learn and recall information. This chapter could easily be an entire book, but the few strategies outlined here can make one's college career both easier and more rewarding.

All learning is hard, and the level of learning in college is so demanding that you can expect it to be a challenge. The strategies in this chapter will not make learning easy, but they will make learning easier, more effective, and certainly less frustrating. The admonition to "work smarter, not harder" certainly applies, although if you really want to be successful in college and beyond, you probably should plan on both working smart and working hard.

Chapter 4
The Art of Communication

T he most important thing to learn in college is how to think clearly about problems. You may wonder how people would know whether you can think clearly, and the answer is simple: you tell them! You do not tell them by saying, "I think clearly," or some similar statement. Instead, you demonstrate that you think clearly by what you say and what you write. However, if your writing is fuzzy, there is no way your clear thoughts can ever be expressed. If you cannot express yourself in words, any brilliant ideas that you may have will be lost in translation.

It is unlikely that you started college without already knowing how to write and speak in public. You learn those things in grade school and high school, but that is just the tip of the iceberg. It is like learning how to move the pieces on a chessboard. Once you learn those rules, you can say that you know how to play chess. However, if you play chess against excellent chess players, they are likely to beat you game after game. Knowing the basics of communication is not the same as being good at communicating. In college, you will have opportunities in your classes to enhance your communication skills, and most universities offer other options to enhance these skills even more. In this chapter, we will briefly review ways to make a substantial improvement in these areas.

Purpose of Communication

There are two purposes for communication. The one that almost everyone is familiar with is to express ideas to one another. A second, often overlooked, purpose of communication is to clarify ideas. We will address both in this chapter but will focus more on clarifying ideas in later chapters.

If you have a good idea but cannot explain it to someone else, you may as well not have the idea. Few people can appreciate a good idea that is not clearly expressed. To be successful at the highest levels, you must have great ideas. But it is just as important to be able to express them in a way that excites other people. You do that in your writing and in your speaking, and as you will learn in this chapter, these are very different skills. Speaking and writing overlap in the sense that you must have a clearly understood and clearly effective idea to be convincing. You must have clear arguments that outline the benefits and advantages of your idea. You must be organized and systematic because if you are not, the idea will seem fuzzy and unworkable. But the way you present the ideas in writing will necessarily be different than the way you present them verbally. Don't believe me? Have you ever had a professor or teacher who simply read from a textbook in class? If so, you have my sympathy. The textbook likely was well-written because publishers are unwilling to put out textbooks that are not clear and understandable. However, the textbook is a poor substitute for a dynamic teacher who brings the textbook to life.

In this chapter, we will be talking about both writing and speaking skills. The chapter is much too short to cover these skills in detail, but I hope you will be able to recognize how each of these skills will be critical to your long-term success.

Enhancing Communication Skills in College

Presumably, by the time you have reached college, you have learned how to write and speak. I say "presumably" because, as a college instructor, I can tell you that many students enter college with very weak communication skills. But for now, let's assume that you do enter college with reasonably good communication skills. Why is it important to improve those communication skills? It is the difference between being adequate and being exceptional. It does not take long to learn the rules of how to play chess. Play chess for a while and you are likely to get reasonably good at it. But if you want to be a strong chess player, you need to both play chess a lot and systematically study chess to improve. You may have no desire to be a chess master, but you do have a desire to be successful in a professional career. Virtually everyone who is successful in a demanding professional career has excellent communication skills. Moreover, it would be hard to even compete for a professional career without solid communication skills.

In the above paragraph, we assumed that you learned basic communication skills before you reached college, but that assumption is not always true. What do you do if your educational background was deficient in this area? Communication skills are like any skill. They are learned, and they are refined with practice. If you believe your writing skills are weaker than you will need, you should take advantage of every opportunity to improve those skills. You do that by using the techniques described later in this chapter. You just need to focus more energy on the task.

What do communication skills buy for you? In the professional world, you almost always meet people through your writing before you meet them personally. The writing may include emails or letters, reports, proposals, and even your résumé. The evidence is overwhelming that people make snap decisions about the qualifications and characteristics of other people. Would you want to go into a meeting with another professional who already assumes that you are not very bright because your introductory letter was so poorly written?

People will hire you or admit you to prestigious programs based on their judgment of your skills. However, there is no way for them to look inside your head to see what skills you have. The only way people can judge your skills is by your presentation of ideas and your history of achievement. If your presentation is sloppy, confusing, and unfocused because you have not learned how to become an excellent writer or an outstanding speaker, most people will conclude that you are not very talented. They will likely decide that you are not good enough to be part of their program. It would be too strong to say that you will never get a second chance to make a good impression, but I can say with confidence that those second chances are rare. You do not want to have a basic deficit in communication skills sabotage the opportunities that come your way.

Improving Your Writing

There is disagreement about the best way to teach basic writing skills, and the way that writing is taught today is different from the way it was taught fifty years ago. For example, most students today are not taught how to diagram sentences the way it was once done in elementary school. I will readily admit that I hated diagramming sentences, and I could see no point in this exercise when I was forced to do it as part of my education. I am not at all sure that it is the best way to teach people to write complex sentences. But I routinely see examples of students who fail to understand that the intended relationship between ideas in their sentences is ambiguous because of the way they structured their sentences.

The way writing is taught today emphasizes communicating ideas rather than the mechanics of grammar and sentence structure. There is nothing conceptually wrong with that approach because the goal of writing is communication. But rules of grammar and sentence structure exist because they help to clarify communication. Regardless of how one was taught to write, the criteria for judging writing are the same. Is it clear what you are saying? Could it be misinterpreted? Would everyone who reads it interpret your ideas the same?

Although there may be disagreement about the best way to teach writing skills, there is little disagreement about the importance of writing skills. There is also surprisingly little disagreement about what constitutes good writing. The pace may be different in a suspenseful thriller versus instructions on how to assemble a computer desk, but to be effective, each type of writing requires clarity that involves selecting the correct words and structuring the sentences in a way that is not only grammatically correct but also easily understood. I have always been intrigued by the fact that good writing is almost invisible. Bad writing, on the other hand, is easy to detect. When writing does not make sense, it frustrates us. We feel like we are being played with. When the writing is clear and understandable, we are focused, not on the writing, but on the message.

Michael Raulin

Learning to improve your writing is just like learning to improve other skills. Teachers can tell you the best ways to write, and books can catalog rules and procedures that will improve your writing. Both help; neither will make you a good writer. What makes a good writer is writing—lots and lots of writing. However, writing by itself is not enough; one needs constructive feedback on the writing to improve. Reading is also important—lots and lots of reading. Reading gives us examples of both good and bad writing. If we are committed to being a better writer, the bad writing will give us great examples of how not to write. Again, our tendency is to ignore good writing, but those who are committed to being excellent writers will go back and look at examples of great writing and study how it is that those authors were able to write with such clarity and were able to construct sentences and paragraphs that grabbed our attention.

A more concrete example may help you to understand this process of learning to write better. Let's focus on a different skill, one that involves physical manipulations. For this example, we will take the game of golf. It only takes one sentence to describe the concept: "The idea is to hit the ball toward a hole and eventually to get the ball into that hole." We can make the description a bit more colorful and a lot more pompous with our selection of words. I remember this definition of golf hanging on the clubhouse wall of my local public course when I was in high school: "Golf is an ineffectual endeavor to put an insignificant pellet into an obscure hole with entirely inadequate weapons." If you are not a golfer, you may not appreciate the emotional content of this latter definition, which every golfer feels at times.

Even if you are not a golfer, you almost certainly realize that the game is more complicated than either of the above definitions imply. You have different clubs, and those clubs differ on how far they are likely to hit the ball and the trajectory of the ball. You have hazards on the course, which you want to avoid, but if you cannot avoid them, they will require different procedures to advance the ball toward the hole. Beyond that, it takes years of practice to master the subtleties of moving a club at the end of a long shaft at speeds sometimes approaching one hundred miles an hour and hitting the ball squarely. However, if you develop the skills and practice them, you can learn to hit that ball consistently in the direction you want (well, reasonably consistently). You may even learn how to do things like curve the ball either right or left as needed to avoid hazards or obstacles. If you play golf, all these principles are obvious. When you watch golf played by professionals on television, you can be amazed at the skill level demonstrated. If you have never played golf, try watching golf for twenty minutes on television. Then borrow a friend's club and a plastic golf ball and try to hit that ball in the backyard to appreciate the complexity of a golfer's skill.

How do golfers at the professional level get so good? It is the same answer given to the New York City tourist asking how to get to Carnegie Hall. Instead of giving directions, the answer is, "Practice, practice, practice!" Only the best professionals play in Carnegie Hall, and they become the best through extensive practice. Professional golfers hit hundreds and even thousands of golf balls every day. They hit most of those golf balls not on a golf course, but on a golf range, where they can hit dozens of different shots to different targets without having to do much walking. If you go to a golf tournament and attend the practice rounds, you will see that these incredibly good golfers practice ten times more shots in the last thirty yards from the hole than they do in the several hundred yards before the hole. Those short shots require finesse, and finesse can only be developed through extensive practice.

The important thing is that top golfers do not just hit golf balls on the range, but they carefully look at the results of each shot and try to associate the results with everything they are doing. So if a shot is not high enough, they adjust something in their swing so the shot will be high enough. If the shot curves when it should not curve, they adjust their swing again so the shot goes in the direction they intended. This process is called deliberate practice. In deliberate practice, one exerts considerable effort not only to do the task but also to constantly observe how effectively the task is being done and adjust when necessary. Deliberate practice is more efficient if you have a good coach who can point out what you are doing wrong and how you may correct it.

The concept of deliberate practice was made famous by the classic research of Ericsson, Krampe, and Tesch-Römer (1993). They studied superstar chess players, golfers, musicians, and superstars from other fields and found something interesting. All these people, who were among the best in their fields, practiced intensely and regularly. Their practice sessions were usually under two hours and so intense that these superstars needed a nap afterward. Casual practice was of little value, but intense deliberate practice was very effective, and research showed that this level of attention during practice works in virtually every field. This has implications for college study. You are far better off studying intensely for shorter times than trying to study for several hours in a row. Be sure to schedule downtime after these intense sessions because you are likely to need that time. However, the results of this study strategy will impress you.

Let's apply these principles to the task of improving your writing. You need to know the basics, and likely you will have learned many of the basics long before you arrived at college. But being a golfer who only knows the basics has a name: hacker. It's not generally a term of endearment. Writers who only know the basics are also hackers, and the quality of their writing is every bit as obvious as the wild and embarrassing shots of the hacker on the golf course. So you need to practice. That means you need to write, and write some more, and write even more. But writing by itself will not necessarily improve your writing. You need feedback on your writing. Golfers have an advantage in that respect. When they swing the club and the ball goes nowhere near where they wanted it to go, that is feedback! They have no trouble recognizing that they must have done something wrong. Unfortunately, writing does not provide that kind of obvious feedback.

You will almost certainly be required to take one or two writing courses in college, which should provide you feedback on your strengths and weaknesses as a writer. If you are lucky, you will be required to write papers in your other courses, and some of those instructors will give you feedback on your writing. Most instructors do not give you feedback on your writing unless it is truly terrible. However, the ones who do give you feedback will help you improve your writing dramatically. But instructors are not the only people capable of giving you good feedback.

Most universities have writing centers that will provide such feedback. Their feedback is usually provided by advanced undergraduate students who happen to be good writers, and incidentally, the experience of trying to improve the writing of other students is a great way to improving your own writing. Check with your instructors to see whether they have any objection to you getting that feedback on a paper before you submit it for the course. Some instructors insist that the entire paper be yours and cannot receive feedback in advance of grading, but many instructors are happy to help you improve your paper by getting feedback on your writing before you submit it. However, once a paper has been submitted for grading, it can always be submitted for critique to the writing center. Their feedback may not improve your grade on that assignment, but it will likely improve your writing and thus improve your grades on future papers.

Another way to improve your writing is to get feedback from other students. Pick students who are pretty good writers and offer to review their papers in exchange for them reviewing your papers. This is an excellent symbiotic relationship because the process results in both students improving their writing. Remember, writing is not the art of stringing words together. Writing is the art of explaining your ideas with clarity and conviction.

You do not learn to write by reading about how to write, although extensive reading of the work of good writers is a valuable way to improve your writing. That said, there are classic books on writing that I strongly recommend. Perhaps the best known is *The Elements of Style* (Strunk, White, & Angell, 1999). This classic was first published in 1935 and updated several times. It manages in less than one hundred pages to identify and explain hundreds of common writing mistakes. I also recommend *On Writing Well* (Zinsser, 2006). Zinsser focuses on nonfiction writing, in which the focus is on being clear and concise. He also does a great job of demonstrating the importance of revision. Great writers routinely go through drafts of everything they write, and each draft is tighter and easier to read. You may read these two books once and then consult them repeatedly until their principles are second nature to you. These two books represent a small financial and time investment that will return huge dividends. They have been on my shelf for decades.

Let me pause for a moment and make an important distinction. If you have nothing worthwhile to say, it does not matter whether you write well. Writing is not a substitute for clear thinking and good ideas. Bad writing can easily hide clear thinking and good ideas to the point that they look weak. In that sense, writing is always secondary to the content. I am going to assume that (1) you are capable of clear and interesting thoughts and (2) you want those thoughts to be expressed with precision. In that case, writing is the way you show off your strong ideas and clear thinking.

Finally, one of the more unappreciated values of writing is that it extends our ability to think about complex issues. Although our brain is amazing, it is clearly limited, and the most important limitation is called working memory. *Working memory* is what we can hold in conscious awareness as we try to put together a solution to a problem. Our working memory has limited capacity, which means that we cannot envision every aspect of a problem when we try to solve it in our heads. However, writing everything down or organizing it in tables or diagrams essentially extends our working memory. We can see all the pieces on paper that we could not see in our limited working memory. We can check all the interactions of the elements and be more confident that we have thought through the problem completely.

There is a corollary to the principle of writing as a way of extending our working memory when trying to solve problems. Students often believe incorrectly that you write a paper by reading and thinking about the topic until you have it clearly organized in your mind. Then you write it down and turn it in. That works only for simple topics. For more complex topics, you need a rough outline of your arguments before you start writing, but then you write and revise to clarify your thinking on the topic. Another common misconception is that you write a paper from front to back. You can start anywhere in a paper, and sometimes starting in the middle works best because you can write a better introduction once you know the direction your paper will take.

To illustrate, I started this book with general ideas based on years of advising students, but in the writing, I added new topics, moved material around, added a couple of chapters, and eliminated or collapsed other chapters to make the arguments flow better. Granted, this book is longer and more complex than a typical college paper, but the principles are the same for developing this book or writing your college papers. Moreover, if you go on to graduate school, you may well be authoring a dissertation at least as long and complicated as this book.

Public Speaking Skills

The point of public speaking, like writing, is to communicate ideas. However, public speaking brings other elements into the process. For many students, the most important other element is the anxiety associated with speaking in front of a group. I spent a good deal of my career treating people with anxiety and anxiety disorders, and I started and ran an anxiety disorders clinic for almost twelve years. I can tell you two things about anxiety. We tend to learn anxiety quickly, and we tend to unlearn it slowly. Many students believe that you do not have to learn to be anxious in public speaking situations because you are anxious right from the beginning. But young children may happily talk and playfully do things in front of people with little distress. The distress that you feel when speaking in front of a class is largely the result of you knowing that you are being judged. We will come back to that point shortly.

Although the rules of communication are identical when you are writing or speaking, the style with which you communicate is different. Writing permits you to express complex ideas in a manner that is precise and understandable. If necessary, the reader may go back over the material to let it sink in. If you use that concept in a speech, you are going to lose the audience. Moreover, it will be painfully obvious that you have lost the audience, and your anxiety may well spiral out of control.

Michael Raulin

You perhaps have heard that when speaking, you should (1) tell the audience what you will be telling them, (2) tell them, and finally, (3) tell them what you told them. Repetition is important in speaking because the listener cannot go back and reread passages as with writing. If you take a perfectly well-written passage from a book and simply read it to the audience, your audience will struggle to understand it. But speaking does have an advantage that you do not have when you are writing. The writer does not get immediate feedback from the reader and so may not realize that the information is not understandable. The speaker does get that feedback. It is a beautiful thing when you can tell in the eyes of the audience that they understand what you are saying. It is even more fun when they agree with what you are saying. However, even when they are not following what you are saying, that feedback allows you to circle back and make your point more clearly.

There is no magic to becoming a good public speaker. In that respect, it is exactly like becoming a good writer. You need to learn the basics, and then you need to practice and practice some more. The practice is best done in a setting in which you can get feedback on how well you are performing. Unfortunately, there is usually less opportunity to get that practice in your college courses than there is opportunity to get practice in writing. Most universities require or strongly recommend at least one course on public speaking. Some universities make this course available online, with students recording their talks and submitting them for evaluation. I do not recommend that you take this option. Part of what you learn in a speech course is how to structure a good talk, but an equally important part is learning to control your anxiety when talking to a group of people. Recording your talks for the teacher deprives you of this second critical element.

If there is an option for additional speech courses, I highly recommend you take that option. I also recommend that you realize that public speaking is only a slightly more formalized version of carrying on a conversation. If you work on a group project with other students and you have ideas to present, view your presentation of those ideas as an opportunity to practice speaking. Try to sell your ideas by presenting them in a clear and convincing manner.

If you are a head of state or a CEO of a corporation, every word you speak in public is likely to have major consequences. A misunderstanding could lead to war or a loss of billions of dollars. Therefore, you are likely to have a formal speech written out, and you will read it, often from a teleprompter. Reading a speech from a teleprompter and making it sound interesting is a skill. For most of us, however, that is not the optimal way of doing public speaking. First, it is inflexible. If we realize from our audience's reaction that what we just said was unclear, we do not have the option of clarifying what we just said. Second, if you are reading, you are not doing the most important thing a speaker can do, which is to make eye contact with the audience. The best speakers speak from notes, but they do not read the notes. Their notes provide the triggers for the ideas they will be expressing. They may have memorized their speech, but it is far more likely that they have only rehearsed the speech using the notes as their guide. This style allows them to focus on the audience, only needing to look down occasionally at their notes to remember the next point they want to make. It also has a secondary advantage we will talk about later.

There is not enough space in this chapter to discuss the details of how to write and give a good talk in a class. That would take an entire book. But there are a few ideas that will help and are relatively easy to learn. Start working on your talk early so you have lots of time to rehearse and modify your presentation. You may start by writing out what you plan to say, but if you do that, be sure to get it down to an outline for the actual presentation. Move to an outline early and rehearse from that outline. Try to rehearse out loud. Wording that seems natural on paper does not always seem natural when spoken aloud. As you do this, you will gradually change your wording to something that either feels more natural or has more punch. Do not be afraid to change things up at this point.

Remember that good talks always have three parts: telling them what you will say, saying it, and telling them what you said. The first part should be less than one hundred words (about one minute). It is good form to introduce the general idea and then tell the audience what aspect of that idea you will focus on. For example, if you are giving a talk on the economic contributors to the Civil War, you may start with something like the following:

> The Civil War was perhaps the most painful and devastating event of our history. It pitted Americans against one another, sometimes even one brother against another brother. The death toll was enormous, and the disruption to our country lasted for decades. Many people believe that the Civil War was fought over slavery, and that is partially true. But I want to focus on another element often overlooked that contributed to the start of the war: a basic disagreement on what should be the basis for our country's economy.

In less than one hundred words, you created a context, convinced the audience that the topic is important, and told them what to expect. I always work hard on this part of the talk because I know that if I capture the audience in the first one hundred words, everything else will be much easier. Another important reason for you to focus hard on this first part of the talk is that if you capture the audience in this first minute, your anxiety is likely to drop dramatically.

Since the first hundred words are so important, you may want to write them out, but once you get familiar through practice, reduce that first paragraph to a few key points. For example, the key points for the about introduction may be as follows:

- Civil War was devasting, pitting Americans against one another
- Many killed; disruptions continued for decades
- Often thought to be fought over slavery
- But economic disagreements also contributed to the start of the war

I am focusing so heavily on the first one hundred words because the same principles will apply to your entire talk. You want to tell a story. More importantly, you want to tell an interesting story. For most of the talk, you will outline the key points of the story and practice telling it out loud in your own words. As you do that, you will see gaps in your story and will fill those in. You will also find words that work better because they make the story more powerful. Once you have the story down, you need to focus on those last one hundred words, which sum up the main points of your story. Those one hundred words are just as important as the first one hundred words because they both sell the story and sell you as the speaker. If you tell a good story and you sell it to the audience at both the beginning and end of your talk, you will look very professional.

You will always have a time limit and staying within that time limit is critical if you want to be impressive. Rehearsing and timing your presentation will give you an idea of how close you are. If your time limit is eight minutes and you are typically taking eleven minutes to get through the material, look for things to cut. In judging what to cut, keep in mind you still want a great story to tell, so do not cut things that contribute to making the story interesting. Never try to stay under the time limit by talking faster. Talking too fast will undo everything else you did right. Also be aware that many people tend to talk faster when they are nervous. If that is true for you, work on rehearsing the proper pacing when you practice your talk. It helps to record the talk and listen to it later to get a sense of whether you are talking too fast for people to follow.

There is an art to public speaking, and part of that art is telling a good story. Putting part of your own personality into your speaking can help you make your story more poignant and convincing. It will also help you with pacing and content. People know instinctively when background information is needed for a story to make sense, and they also know that talking too fast or slow will make a story harder to follow. I wish I could give you advice on exactly how to develop your own personal style in speaking. However, that is something you pick up with practice, and you will likely not always get the balance correct. You want to view this area of development, like every area, with a growth mindset.

I have three final points for your rehearsal strategy. The first is to spread the rehearsal out. Rehearse once or twice a day for approximately thirty minutes, even when you are still refining your talk. Practice over several days. You already learned that this strategy of spreading out your practice dramatically improves your learning. A second advantage of spreading out your practice is that you will hear things that can be improved if you walk away from the speech for a while before rehearsing again. Finally, it is helpful to record your talk during rehearsal. You will be amazed at what you are able to hear and correct when you have a recording of your talk to work with. Audio recordings work well, but video recordings are even more effective. The video will show you exactly how the audience will see you when it is your turn to present.

The second point I want to make is that almost every speech has natural sections, and most people will rehearse each of the sections independently. That is a bad idea because when you get to the end of a section, it may not be obvious what comes next. To avoid this, when you are practicing a section, run the practice past the end of the section into the beginning of the next section. This is a small point, but it will prevent you from freezing during your talk because you cannot find in your notes what comes next.

I mentioned earlier the issue of anxiety when speaking in public. If the idea of public speaking makes you anxious, you are not alone. If you never get anxious with public speaking, you are missing something valuable. Anxiety drives us to engage in behavior that reduces our anxiety. If we get anxious around public speaking, we are highly motivated to prepare well so we can give an excellent speech. You may be surprised to learn that great speakers do get anxious; their anxiety prompts them to prepare, and they have learned to manage the anxiety so it does not interfere with their performance. This principle applies to just about every situation in which one is being judged. Preparation both improves performance and reduces anxiety.

We talked earlier about the anxiety that many students feel when speaking in public. One of the best ways to manage anxiety is to focus your attention away from the anxiety. However, we are terrible at focusing our attention away from things. Let me give you a quick and silly example. Silly examples work well because they are easy to remember.

I want you to imagine an elephant in the room—a real elephant and not a figurative one, and not just a normal elephant. I want you to imagine an elephant that is a bright neon color. Now, *do not think of that elephant.* Wipe the thought of that elephant out of your mind. If you were visualizing that neon elephant, you probably realized that the more you tried not to think about that elephant, the more you thought about it. But try a different approach: think about something else right now. Think about the most important person in your life and what he or she looks like. Chances are that elephant goes away all by itself once you focus on something else.

The "something else" you need to focus on when you are doing public speaking is the audience. You are speaking to the audience, so it is easy to focus on them. Think of them as friends you are speaking to, and focus on them, because you want them to understand what you are saying. The more you focus on them, the less you will focus on any anxiety you may be feeling. I do not have to tell you what happens when you focus on your anxiety. As soon as you notice that your voice is cracking or your hands are shaking or that you are sweating, the anxiety spirals out of control. It may not be possible to ignore your anxiety, but with a little practice you can learn to focus on something other than the anxiety, such as the audience. It also helps to remind yourself that you are much more aware of your personal anxiety than your audience is likely to be. Most people in the audience will completely miss the signs of your anxiety.

Earlier I talked about the advantage of learning to talk from notes rather than writing out a speech and reading it. One advantage is that speaking from notes allows you to focus on the audience, looking for clues of how well they understand your presentation. That information can allow you to make minor modifications in your talk when many audience members are confused about a point you are making. But there is another advantage of being able to watch the audience. It focuses your attention away from any anxiety you may be feeling. Many students discover that once they get into their speech, their anxiety drops dramatically because everything is going smoothly, and the audience is responding positively.

By the way, if you are anxious about public speaking, the hardest time is just before you must speak. If several students are speaking in front of you, you are likely to feel your anxiety grow while they are speaking. However, if you focus on what the earlier speakers are saying, you will not be focusing on the anxiety building inside of you, and so the anxiety will not spiral out of control. One way to reduce your anxiety is to volunteer to go first if you can. That way, you do not have to sit through other talks as your own anxiety builds.

Finally, you can reduce your anxiety by making sure the technology is working before you are in front of the audience. It can be very disconcerting when it is your turn to talk and the PowerPoint slides are not working. If you can, check everything out before you present. A related issue is having a backup in mind. For example, if you had planned on downloading your PowerPoint presentation and you discover that the computer in the classroom is not connected to the Internet, you are screwed. Having a flash drive with your presentation can be your backup.

Chapter Summary

Many students hate writing papers and hate giving talks in class even more. Consequently, they go out of their way to select courses that do not include papers or talks. That is a terrible mistake because the ability to communicate effectively is second only to the ability to think clearly in predicting how well you will do in the future.

Communication is a skill, and like every skill, it benefits from practice and coaching. If you know the basics of grammar and sentence structure and have a reasonable vocabulary, you can become a good writer with practice. With sufficient practice and attention to detail, you can become an excellent writer, and the things you write will boost your career.

The anxiety that convinces many people that they could never be a good speaker decreases the more you speak, provided that your experience with speaking is not traumatic. With some instruction and practice, you will avoid the trauma and, over time, will improve to the point of being impressive. Anxiety is a state that simply indicates that you are unsure that you can handle the current situation. The better you get at public speaking, the less anxious you will be because you will know that you can give an impressive talk. The more thoroughly you prepare a talk, the more confident you will be that it will be good, and therefore, the less anxious you will be.

The primary goal of college education and advanced study is to teach you to think more clearly and solve increasingly more demanding problems. However, if you cannot communicate your solutions to those problems, you will be unable to convince people of your talent and potential.

Chapter 5
Associate Ideas with People

Y ou probably noticed in your textbooks that there are either footnotes or names in parentheses that identify the individuals responsible for the ideas or information being presented. If you are like most students, including me in college, you have learned to ignore these. You ignore them because there is little point in learning that information. You expect the examinations for the course to focus on facts and ideas and not on the people responsible for these facts or ideas. Frankly, that is a safe assumption with most undergraduate courses. Instructors in undergraduate classes typically do not question students about the names of the individuals responsible for the content in their course.

By graduate school, however, the names become more important. You notice them, you process them, and you connect those ideas to the people who created them. You also become more interested in how they created those ideas because, by the time you start graduate school, you are committing yourself to being one of those people as part of your career. Linking the ideas that you learn to the people who created those ideas turns a list of facts and theories into a good story. As you learned earlier, people remember good stories much better than they remember individual facts. Within the context of a good story, people can easily remember hundreds of specific facts and, more importantly, can recall those facts when they need them later.

In many disciplines, the amount of material in a core course has grown so much in the past few decades the textbooks have more than doubled in size. The reason is simple: we know so much more now, and much of that material is so important that it needs to be in these basic texts. However, the courses have typically remained the same length and are worth the same number of credits. Consequently, textbook publishers have started to provide more textbooks that have less detail. The idea is that a 450-page textbook is much less intimidating to both students and faculty than say a 750-page textbook. However, the shorter text may appear less intimidating, but it often is more difficult to read. The number of facts presented is almost identical in the two texts, but the longer text allowed the author to weave the facts into interesting stories that are easier to remember. Consequently, students often find the longer text to be more interesting and easier to follow.

I know that different fields have different styles for their textbooks. In some fields, it is common to emphasize the history of the field and how the people who created the field did their work. In other fields, textbooks focus only on the material and what you need to know about the material, rarely spending more than a token amount of time on the history and the people who made the field possible. I personally think that is unfortunate, but I understand that if the norm is to cover specific material in a limited amount of time, sometimes you must make some tough decisions.

Examples of History Organizing the Learning

For many years, I have enjoyed audio and videotaped lectures from The Teaching Company, which are part of the Great Courses Series. This company finds the best college instructors and has them give their course on tape. I am not here to endorse any products, but I will tell you I truly enjoy these courses. Their instructors are exceedingly good at explaining material, and they are exceptionally well organized so that the information is presented in a logical, easy-to-follow manner. They are passionate about their area, and their passion is obvious and infectious. One thing that has always struck me is that, without exception, these outstanding instructors present their material as a series of stories, and the stories usually revolve around the people who created the field. In their presentation, the stories are not historical footnotes. They are the structure on which all the information from the field is organized.

It would be foolish for me to say that all teaching should be done this way. It would be foolish for me to say that all textbooks should be written emphasizing the people responsible for the field.

It is certainly possible to learn things without knowing how the information is tied to specific individuals. Frankly, for most of my college life, that is the way I learned. However, I find now that it is much easier for me to learn the material by emphasizing the history and the people responsible for how things developed. Once I learn the material, it is much easier for me to recall it if the material has been presented in this kind of story format. I try to incorporate this information into my teaching and into my writing. It is possible that the Great Courses that I have completed is a biased sample. But my interests in such courses are broad; I have completed more than one hundred of the Great Courses in a dozen different fields since I learned about the series. Every course had a series of stories, and within those stories was embedded information that I not only remember, but also could use in my own work.

Organizing Information around Stories

Most people are not very good at learning facts. That fact probably makes you feel better. You are not alone. We can learn facts, but it takes tremendous effort, and the facts that we learn are not stable. However, we are great at remembering stories, and within those stories, we can easily organize dozens or even hundreds of individual facts. Moreover, if those stories are well-formed, we can use them to generate the facts that we have forgotten because that information is going to be critical to the story.

The best instructors do not repeat the information in the textbook without putting it into a context that will help students to remember it. That context is often a story of either how something works or how we figured out how it works. It is amazing how much information you can organize within a story.

You do not have to have an instructor who understands the value of stories for you to use the principle of organizing information in the form of stories. You can build your own stories by asking the right questions to fill in the gaps of the story. Do not just accept a statement that this is the best procedure. Ask why it is the best procedure. Ask what criteria were used to determine whether it is the best procedure. Ask how these criteria are used to judge other procedures in related areas. You will be amazed at how many of these questions can be answered in five minutes on the Internet if you formulate the correct questions. You will also be amazed at how impressed most instructors will be when you ask such questions. (As an aside, you will also run across occasional instructors who not only hate addressing such questions but also take it out on students who are willing to ask them. You probably are not going to be able to change those instructors, but you can write them off by saying to yourself, "They should probably be looking for another occupation.")

There is a secondary advantage to learning the skill of creating the story that will help you remember the information in a course. Stories have plots, and those plots revolve around key issues. Those key issues are critical concepts that need to be understood. They go well beyond the facts. They are the elements that are the difference between dropping a few interesting words and understanding what you are talking about. In other words, knowing the stories will give you a deeper understanding of the concepts.

Supplementing Your Learning with Historical Information

The workload in college can be overwhelming, so the idea of increasing the workload by adding something else is not appealing. Nevertheless, I want to argue that being interested in, and focusing on, the historical background of the information that you are learning will pay dividends. First, it will prepare you for graduate and professional school. In college, the focus is often on learning the basics, but in post-college education, the focus is on understanding the field and the directions in which the field is moving. The transition to this level of learning is much easier for those students who have developed a healthy interest in the historical development of their field. But an advantage of focusing on such historical information as an undergraduate is that it will help you make better-informed decisions about the direction you want your career to go.

The second reason for focusing on the historical background in a field is that such focus gives you insights that you will not get any other way. We have already talked about how putting information into a story helps you remember the information, but the historical story will help you understand how people created the field and advanced it. Once you get focused on the stories, it will become clear that most fields are dependent on a relatively small number of amazing individuals. Those individuals will become the focus of your reading because their ideas are so valuable, insightful, and helpful to your understanding. Universities have often emphasized the importance of reading great works, although in my humble opinion that emphasis has been decreasing over time. Great works are great because they have great ideas, and there are great works in every field. Learning to recognize the authors of those great works will focus your energy on learning from the best.

I love teaching college, and I love students who enjoy college. I believe in the value of college as an institution that fosters learning and the love of learning. But my philosophy of life has always been: "If I do my job well, I work myself out of a job." I try hard to make the information in my classes understandable and interesting, but my goal is to encourage students to find their own ways of learning and advancing their skills. Reading a book is almost never a waste of time; reading an excellent book written by a true scholar can be a wonderful use of your time.

You may not think of it this way, but writing is a way of shifting communication in both time and space. You do not have to be in a classroom with someone who has great ideas if they have published books about those ideas. You do not even have to be alive at the same time. Their ideas can inspire your ideas. Their ideas can challenge your ideas. Their ideas can inspire you to develop your own ideas. The key to all of this is learning to appreciate the people whose work can do that for you. In most textbooks, there will be names in parentheses scattered throughout the book. Those names are citations to articles or books written about the subject. Most students develop the skill of skipping over that parenthetical information. Do not skip over it. You do not need to memorize the names but notice when certain names keep coming up again and again. Those are people you probably want to learn more about, and in the process, you will likely dramatically improve your understanding of the material.

Chapter Summary

In a TV show so old that most of you have probably never heard of it (Dragnet), the police officer would often tell witnesses, "Just give me the facts." College courses sometimes feel that way because there is so little time in class and so much material to cover and because textbooks have had to leave material out to prevent overwhelming students. Facts by themselves are hard to remember. Moreover, the facts by themselves are often of little value other than winning trivia contests. They do not become truly valuable until you organize them and integrate them with other facts and ideas. Students that focus on putting the facts together and understanding the story behind them tend to (1) remember the facts better and (2) understand the relationship of the facts to other ideas and other facts.

Stories have characters, and the characters in your college courses are the people whose ideas shaped the field. If your goal is to be one of the best people in a field, you need to get to know those individuals who shape the field. You may not have the opportunity to take their courses or study with them in graduate school, but you can read their ideas and learn from them, and you do not have to have that material assigned to you in of course for you to read it. In high school, most students simply learn what is presented to them. In college, most students focus only on what is covered in courses. But if your goal is to go beyond college and shape a field, you need to take the initiative to identify the work that is worth reading. Those who will shape the field in the future will build their ideas on the work of those who shaped it in the past.

Chapter 6
The Five-Year Plan

Y ou are about to start college. Your five-year plan is obvious. You want to finish college and move on. What more do you need? Thinking five years ahead seems unnecessary and may even feel impossible. If you are reading this as a typical college freshman, five years is more than a quarter of your life. I hope to convince you in this chapter that (1) it is possible to think five years ahead, and (2) there are incredible advantages to thinking that way.

Think back five years and think of all that has happened to you in the past five years—it is an amazing number of things. Now switch your perspective. Imagine yourself five years ago looking forward. Could you have predicted all the things that happened to you? Could you have predicted even half of the things that happen to you? If you could not predict them, how could you possibly plan for them?

A Sample Five-Year Plan

A plan is not a list of the things you intend to do. That is called a to-do list, and it is very handy to get through a few days of activities. A plan focuses on the bigger picture that will guide your day-to-day decisions. For example, your five-year plan as an entering college freshman may include items such as these:

(1) Use the first year to complete the core courses in your intended major, which will open advanced courses for you.

(2) Use the first two years to complete all the general education requirements so that you have the flexibility to specialize in your last two years of college.

(3) As much as possible, use the general education requirements to sample areas that may be more

interesting to you than your planned area of concentration.

(4) Do not think just in terms of required courses but rather in terms of developing necessary skills, such as critical thinking, communication (written and oral), and applying your knowledge to real-world problems.

(5) Develop relationships with people more knowledgeable about your field than you and learn from them what you can about career opportunities and the pathway to those opportunities. That may include your academic advisor and faculty members, especially in your major, but it could also include advanced undergraduates or graduate students.

(6) Go beyond good grades in courses and get experiences that will make you stand out for jobs or advanced training after you graduate. This may include working in research labs or doing volunteer activities. It could easily include assuming leadership roles that will establish your competence and the trust of those who evaluate your competence.

(7) If your career goals involve specialized training after your undergraduate degree, begin to learn about what is needed to be competitive early in your college career. Then, plan your college career so that you have the experiences that will maximize your competitiveness. (In general, it is hard to be competitive for graduate programs if you start the process of being competitive during your junior year.)

(8) Keep an open mind, and constantly ask about whether your goals have changed. A career decision you made at the age of sixteen is almost certainly based on limited information. Perhaps at the age of nineteen, with much more information, it is time to

question whether that original choice is still the optimal choice for you. Changing career directions can be frightening because it feels like you have wasted your time. However, making the right decision now is much more important than committing to a forty-year career in a field that does not excite you.

(9) The advantage of focusing the early years of your education on general education requirements is that it allows you to gather the information that may lead you in different directions. Moreover, this strategy will open your schedule in later years to be able to change your major or minor and still graduate on time.

(10) Focus on building the attitudes that will make you successful. Those attitudes may include hard work, resilience, and a sense that with enough work you will succeed. Do not expect things to be easy, and when they are hard, view it as a challenge to overcome.

(11) Build relationships with people who have similar attitudes and values. It is fine to party occasionally, but if your closest friends only want to party, chances are they will influence you in negative ways. This involves finding the balance that allows you to succeed yet take care of yourself physically and emotionally.

(12) Build and maintain strong friendships. Friendships are a two-way street. Friends provide support, information, and recreation. When things are bad, they can keep us grounded. But the expectation is that you will provide the same support to them.

(13) Find and develop nonacademic activities that enhance your character and help you maintain a balance in your life. Depending on your personality,

skills, and temperament, these could include sports, hobbies, social groups, or religious affiliations.

(14) Plan on seriously reconsidering this plan in two years. It is possible that the plan will still be relevant, in which case you will simply extend the plan out two more years. But the norm is that situations change, and you may change too. If so, revising the plan is in order.

Your first five-year plan may look a lot like this one, just a little more than a single page. Note that there is not a single "to-do item" in the entire plan. Also note that the norm is to update your five-year plan, not every five years, but rather every two years. No five-year plan ever lasts five years, although elements of the plan may last much longer than that. The reason you have a five-year horizon is to help you to think more long term about your goals. It is so easy as a college freshman to focus on your courses and then on the courses that you will take next semester. However, if you are not thinking past college, you probably are not making optimal decisions for yourself.

Elements of a Five-Year Plan

The sample plan above looks straightforward, but it is more complicated than it looks. If you are reading this book as a new college freshman or someone about to start college, you probably learned some things from the plan. For example, you may not have realized that there are certain courses that must be taken before you are allowed to take other courses or that a college program requires general education courses. If someone hands you your course plan, you do not have to worry about learning these things. But if you want a custom plan that fits your needs, you will have to do the research to discover the details that need to be part of the plan. In this section, we will talk about the elements of the plan and how you will go about gathering the information to formulate the plan and modify it as you move along.

Finding Information

Successful people know how to solve problems, and part of solving problems is finding and utilizing relevant information. The work you put into planning the next few years is one of the most important exercises in building a set of skills that will serve you well no matter what career you choose.

The trick is not just to find the information you need, but rather to synthesize that information in a way that allows you to do careful planning. It is easy to know what is required to get a degree. Every university publishes that information. Moreover, they often try to simplify the information by creating tables with tentative schedules so that most students do not need to think much about what to take when. It is great that the university has sought to provide that information in a convenient form. However, buried in that information are the principles that the experts used for creating those tentative schedules. If you want to excel, you need to extract the principles from the examples.

It is not difficult to find out why colleges require general education courses. Most colleges make that clear in their materials. A well-educated professional is not only an expert in one or more areas but also has the broader perspective that one can only gain by being more widely read. Okay, I know that sounds like a silly excuse for making you take more courses than you need. Frankly, if you do not select those courses with reasonable care, it may indeed be a collection of courses that does little for you but helps the university extract more tuition money. The definition of a well-educated professional on which general education requirements rest may be widely accepted but is often unsatisfying. What makes it unsatisfying is that it does not tell you why the broader education has value. Once you understand the answer to that question, you have the tools to plan your own curriculum.

The best way to get information is to find someone who is likely to know it and ask them. The most important word in this sentence is *likely*. Many people who should know the answer to certain questions often do not, or alternatively, they once knew but have long since forgotten. The best strategy for getting information is to ask the right questions. Almost all questions that are important involve the word *why*. While those are often the correct questions, the wording is problematic. Here is a trick that will serve you well for your entire life, and it comes from my training in clinical psychology. If you ask a question that starts with *why*, you will almost always make the person defensive and therefore will obtain less valuable information. Think about it. When someone asks you why you did something, your likely response is something like, "Why, what did I do wrong?" That is a perfectly reasonable response, but unfortunately, it also uses the word *why* and will make the other person more defensive.

Virtually every question that starts with why can be reworded to get you a better answer and avoid making the person defensive. For example, asking your advisor the question, "What is the purpose of general education?" does not challenge the person you are asking and elicits the rationale for the requirement. You can make the question even more effective by playing dumb. You can do this by prefacing your question with, "I guess I do not understand the logic behind general education." Now, the person you are talking to understands that you want to understand the logic and that you believe understanding the logic will make you a better student. What a great way to motivate people to help you.

People who ask great questions tend to get excellent information. Perhaps even more importantly, people who ask great questions tend to impress those individuals being questioned. Also, most people love to hear themselves talk, so asking questions is a great way to make people feel special. In grade school and high school, most students believe that smart people are the ones who can answer questions. By college and beyond, the most impressive people are the ones who know how to formulate the best questions, which are the questions that are worth the energy it will take to find the answers.

Questioning is an art and a skill, and the more you do it, the better you will get at it. In time, you will get good enough that you will be able to ask great questions without having to think about it. Initially, however, you will likely have to plan your questions in advance. If you are meeting with an advisor, think about what information you want and why that information is important. Then translate those goals into clearly worded questions.

When planning your questions, remember that it is rare that a single question will elicit all the information you want. If you think clearly about what you want, you can formulate a series of predictable questions that will get you what you need. An example may be asking the question about the purpose of general education. You can use the question we formulated above and elicit the proper response. However, it would be a rare individual whose answer is entirely satisfactory. What you do is follow up with questions that make it increasingly clear what you are after. You may ask, for example, "How can I use general education to enhance my own preparation for a career and beyond?" Again, even the best-worded questions can be uncomfortable for some individuals, but by creating a context for the question, you can decrease their discomfort and therefore increase the likelihood that they will help. For example, you could start by thanking them for their answer to the question of the purpose of general education before asking how you can use that information to your maximum advantage. Do not worry about playing dumb as a strategy when asking questions. If you ask good questions and even better follow-up questions, no one will think you are dumb.

We have focused most of this section on getting information by asking people who should know the information. This is an excellent strategy, but it does not always work. Many people who should know the answers to such questions have never actually thought about those questions and therefore are unlikely to have good answers. Do not get discouraged; ask others the same questions. You will discover that your questions are fine but only some people know the answers to them. You will also discover that different people have different perspectives and therefore give you different answers, and the fact that such differences of opinion exist is very helpful as well.

Asking questions is helpful, but it is not the only way to get information. There is an amazing amount of information at your fingertips. You already knew that, right? It is called the Internet. The Internet is amazing, but to use the Internet effectively you must be skeptical. It is easy to post something on the Internet, and some of the material on the Internet is inaccurate. But a good rule of thumb when searching for information on the Internet is to look for consistency across sites. This does not guarantee the accuracy of the information, because sometimes bad information is repeated by other sites. However, it is a reasonably effective tool.

The odds are good that the university you are attending has a website with thousands of pages of information. Spend time getting to know the university by reading some of that information. Better yet, spend more time reading the websites of other universities to see how they explain the resources available to their students. You may well find a university that explains things much better than your own university. Remember, information is not just knowing facts; information means understanding those facts. Good writers will give you the facts and explain them, but not everyone is a good writer. You want to become a good reader, which means you keep asking for the explanation and not just the facts. You want the word *why* to be your response to almost everything you read, although you learned earlier in this section that you will not be using that word when you ask follow-up questions.

Formulating a Plan Based on that Information

It makes sense that you should gather information first and then formulate a plan. In general, that is what I recommend. However, it is common for these two steps to be iterative. You gather information and formulate a tentative plan, and then you gather more information and revise the plan.

The other issue in formulating a plan is that the plan usually has several units that are only loosely associated. Using the example of the five-year plan for college freshmen outlined above, the units include general education, your major and your minor, planning for graduate school in your career, building the right attitudes, and developing strategies that will provide the balance and support you need to be successful. The elements in your plan ten years from now will overlap some of these elements but will often have unique features. The information gathering becomes increasingly more complex over time because there will be fewer constraints on your behavior. It is relatively easy to plan a college curriculum because the university outlines the expectations. However, the real world does not divide itself into classes and semesters, and the criteria for success become more challenging because they depend more heavily on values. Some people will emphasize the importance of a balanced family life, whereas others prefer to focus on rapid advancement in their career. Neither value is best; people have a right to select the values that are most important for them. You do not need to justify your values to other people, and you should not expect other people to justify their values to you.

Implicit in the previous paragraph is the idea that one source of the information to guide your plan is your values. Ignoring our values in planning our life is perilous. We will all experience setbacks in life, and those setbacks will be distressing. But in the long run, we are likely to be able to handle such setbacks, and some people thrive on setbacks. But not living up to our values typically results in an existential discomfort that is much harder to address. We have talked about values several times in this book, and we will do more of it in later chapters. The reason is that values are so important to planning our lives, and unlike other things in life, there is no easy way to know how to discover your personal values. I am not sure what you will get if you type the question, "What are my personal values?" into Google, but I suspect it will not be terribly helpful.

Constantly Verifying the Information

Your plan should never be set in stone because things change. Some changes may be especially powerful, such as changes in our values. But other changes can be subtle because of small changes in information. We tend to naïvely think of information as facts, and we think of facts as stable. Some facts are stable, such as the age at which you start college. But other facts change. We are in an economy that is changing so rapidly that it is hard to predict what the hot careers will be a decade from now. It is reasonable to believe that many careers that look good now may not be good options ten years from now because of changes in the economy. I worked my way through college driving a truck; it was a good living, and it easily paid all my college expenses. Right now, as I write this, there is a shortage of truck drivers, and so the pay is excellent. But what if the self-driving technology currently under development is applied to the trucking industry? Could the number of truck drivers needed be cut in half in less than five years? It certainly could. Supply and demand principles are currently keeping truck driving salaries high; cut demand by 50 percent, and the salaries will drop dramatically.

When you gather information, it is helpful to categorize the information as stable or potentially unstable. Some information is so potentially volatile that the idea of a five-year plan is foolish. Fortunately, most information is less volatile and can be used to guide reasonable decisions for at least a few years. It is a good idea to routinely review the accuracy of the data on which with your five-year plan was originally formulated.

Determining a Timetable

A plan is always a combination of goals and timetables for achieving those goals. We will discuss both in this section.

A goal is a statement of what you wish to achieve. Sometimes, elements of the timetable are part of the goal. For example, a goal may be to save enough for retirement so you are financially ready to retire at sixty. A financial planner can help you decide how much money that is, but that decision will rest on other things, such as the lifestyle you wish to maintain in retirement.

Goals should be specific so that it is clear whether you have achieved the goal. In fact, a good rule of thumb for goals is expressed with the acronym SMART: Make your goals specific, measurable, achievable, relevant, and time bound. The goal, "Become a better person," is fine but virtually useless. How would you know if you achieved that goal? How would others know if you achieved that goal? How can you prove on your résumé that you have achieved that goal? A better goal may be, "Become the kind of employee my boss can depend on." There are likely to be concrete examples of behaviors that would demonstrate that you have achieved that goal. For example, you likely would have been given more responsibilities, would have recorded successes on demanding assignments, and would have been given promotions or raises to reward you for your work. Note that effective goals routinely can be translated into a series of easily documented achievements. If you can easily answer the question, "How will I know when I have achieved this goal?" then you have a good goal to work toward. The likely reason most New Year's resolutions fail is that they are almost always too vague. Make your New Year's resolutions SMART (specific, measurable, achievable, relevant, and time bound), and you are much more likely to be successful.

Goals can be as simple as setting the alarm for 7:00 AM and getting up when the alarm goes off or as complex as starting a company and building it until it has more than one thousand employees. The goals that you state in your five-year plan should be somewhere between these two. If you can achieve the goal in one day, it is really a to-do list item. If the goal will take a lifetime, is more an aspiration than a goal. Most goals in a five-year plan should take one to three years to fully achieve, but good planners will almost certainly expand those goals into a series of smaller goals to be able to monitor progress. For example, the five-year plan for college freshmen may include the two-year goal of completing the general education requirements, but that goal can be expanded to include the subgoals of completing each of those requirements.

Breaking a major goal into a series of subgoals is a great management strategy. If you include deadlines for each of the subgoals, it is an even better management strategy because you can monitor your progress as you move along. One advantage of breaking larger goals into subgoals is it becomes easier to plan and create a timetable for the completion of the subgoals.

There is an important principle in planning how long a task will take that I learned from my major professor when I started graduate school. He told me that I should list every step that needed to be done to complete the task and list the maximum amount of time it should take to complete each of those steps. Then he told me I should double that number. He said my estimate would still be unreasonably optimistic but at least in the ballpark. He was correct.

Although timetables are difficult to establish and even more difficult to maintain, they do serve an important purpose. They give us an idea of how well we are doing in moving toward our goals. When we are behind and have a firm deadline, we need to modify our priorities so we can get more time and attention to focus on our primary goals. Timetables also serve an important secondary goal. Few people can stay highly motivated for months or years on a particular goal. We need to be reinforced regularly and completing subgoals is reinforcing. We feel like we are making progress, and that motivates us to work harder.

Mixing Goals and Strategies

Having clearly defined goals is important because they represent the guideposts by which we mark progress. However, goals by themselves are not sufficient. We need specific strategies for achieving each of our goals. The goal is what we want to achieve, and the strategy is the means to achieve it.

I encourage people to integrate goals and strategies. Goals are less intimidating if you know how you will achieve them; focusing on strategies forces one to identify the reasonableness of goals and the impediments one is likely to face in achieving those goals. Assume for the moment that your goal is the completion of a major project, such as a senior thesis, as an undergraduate. You know you want to complete the thesis in time to graduate. Suppose that as part of the study, you want to interview fifty people and use what you learn to answer specific questions. Suppose further that your work on the interview suggests that it will take an average of ninety minutes for each interview and another sixty minutes to evaluate the interview. You recognize that this is a major task requiring significant time (2.5 hours times 50 people equals 125 hours). On the surface, this looks doable. If you set aside 10 hours a week for one semester, you should be able to complete the task.

Remember the concept of how to plan the time needed to complete a major project? Our computation was 125 hours, but that was assuming that everything went as planned. It did not consider the time it takes to schedule people and remind them of the importance of showing up. It did not include the people who failed to show up and had to be rescheduled. It did not include the interviews that had to be cut short or rescheduled because of time commitments that either you or your interviewees had. It did not include the blocks of time that were not large enough to schedule ninety-minute interviews. It also did not include the weeks that you had two exams and three papers due and therefore did not have the time to interview anyone. It did not include the weeks that it was hard to schedule anyone because vacation was about to start. Finally, it did not include the times that you set aside for scoring the interviews during which you were so tired you could not focus. Perhaps 250 hours is a better estimate, although I would guess that it is probably overly optimistic. Your strategy of interviewing fifty people over a semester is starting to look unworkable. Perhaps an alternative strategy, such as using an online survey with one hundred subjects makes more sense.

The above example illustrates how a careful analysis of your strategy to complete a goal may lead you to reconsider the goal or modify it. But you do not have to rely on only your own analysis. Get the advice of knowledgeable people, such as your academic supervisor, to supplement your analysis.

In the example, the analysis was handled before formalizing the goal, but there are times when the early experience with a task forces us to rethink our plan. Perhaps you expect to have the time to interview fifty people for your thesis, but you discover that the only times you have a room available to conduct the interview is a time that few of your subjects are available. What do you do? If you cannot get another interview space, your plan to interview fifty people may be unworkable, so you need to adjust. The important issue here is that adjustment is easier if you recognize the difficulty early and explore options before you have invested too much effort into a process that will not be workable. I recently ran across a quotation from a Fortune 500 CEO that is applicable here. "Be stubborn on vision, flexible on details." There is a lot of wisdom in those seven words.

Revising Your Plan

No plan lasts forever, and a five-year plan almost never lasts five years. So why do I call it a five-year plan? Five years is a reasonable increment for laying out your life. Life is so unpredictable that trying to plan further out would be a work of fiction. Planning your life one year at a time fails to provide the direction for long-term achievement. A five-year plan gives you a sense of where you are headed for a year or two or three. It focuses you on the details that you need to do to get to your goals. However, you can also predict that the unpredictability of life will gradually make any five-year plan obsolete.

Your plan will need revision at some point. How much revision and when to do those revisions is up to you. I recommend a semiannual review of how the plan is working for you. That is often enough to detect deviations from the assumptions behind the plan that are significant enough to warrant rethinking the plan. Of course, if there is a major change in your life, a careful evaluation of your plans is in order. If you are about to get married or divorced or if one of your children is experiencing significant health difficulties, you may want to look carefully at the plan. If there are opportunities too good to ignore, you may want to take advantage of them and adjust your plan as necessary. Perhaps there are changes that will block you from the goals you have set for yourself. Perhaps other changes will make previously abandoned goals relevant again.

Revising a five-year plan does not mean starting from scratch. If it was a good plan, the most important elements may not require changes. Presumably, your values will remain unchanged even as the world around you changes. Within those values, however, the best means for you to live up to them could change and require refocusing your goals. If you find yourself focusing on values in a new plan, it would be wise to ask yourself why you are questioning those values. Perhaps what you want out of life has indeed changed, but occasionally the problem is that you find yourself frustrated by not being able to achieve the goals you have set. Some goals may have a short shelf life. For example, if you want a big family but have not yet married at the age of fifty, it is unlikely that you will get married and have several children. If you have always wanted to be a professional football player, and you have not yet been drafted at the age of thirty, you may want to discard that goal.

You will not achieve every goal you listed in your five-year plan. Some people would argue that if you do achieve every goal in your five-year plan, your goals were unreasonably low. The purpose of goals is to enhance your performance. If the goals are so high so that failure is inevitable, the goals become an impediment. They simply discourage your effort. If the goals are too low, you never get a chance to show your capabilities. I wish I could tell you exactly how to set those goals. The best I can do is to tell you that failing to reach all your goals is normal. In general, you will be judged by what you have accomplished and how you treat others. Most people will have no idea what goals are in your five-year plan.

Following Your Plan

Making your five-year plan will be a challenge; following it will be even more difficult. A good plan is easier to follow than a bad plan, but that does not mean it will be easy. A good plan gives you guidance without trapping you in a narrow perspective. Let us take a simplified example. You are in Phoenix, Arizona, and your plan is to go straight north to Canada. That plan is fine but lacks flexibility. What do you do when you run into the Grand Canyon? Going straight north means climbing down into the canyon, crossing the Colorado River, climbing back up the canyon wall, and proceeding to Canada. It may make a whole lot more sense to move east or west until you find an easier way to turn back north. In the same way, a five-year plan sometimes needs to be modified when you hit a wall (or in this case, a mile-deep canyon).

Chapter Summary

A five-year plan not only provides guidance and direction, but also allows you to check off progress toward your goals. However, things change, and consequently, we need to revise our life plans frequently. The process of creating the plan encourages us to think of our values, resources, and goals. There is nothing magical about a five-year plan. It is long enough to force us to think longer term, but short enough that we can make reasonable guesses about what we are likely to face. However, we should not wait five years before we revise our five-year plan. Instead, we should look at the plan at least every couple of years and revise it as necessary.

Section II
Academic Success

I have spent most of my life in academia because, frankly, I love it. I love learning, and as an academic, I am being paid to learn. They pay me to learn because they expect me to be on the cutting edge so I can teach cutting-edge material to students. I believe in the value of learning. I believe that education can be the foundation for success. But I also recognize that there is a huge difference between academic environments and the real world. There is a reason they call universities ivory towers. In this section, I will focus on how to optimize your performance in college and beyond, but I will do it in the context that your college experiences are only the ticket to admission to the real world.

Let me also point out that college is not for everyone, and that college is not the only pathway to success. Skilled tradespeople will always be in demand, and careers in the trades can be both satisfying and lucrative. I will not be covering those career paths in this book simply because it is not the focus of the book. However, there are several excellent books that will introduce you to various trades (e.g., Kitts, 2019; Lussier & Lussier, 2019). What I will point out is that the college pathway is not inherently different from the way people in the trades build their careers. Granted, people in the trades do not usually attend formal classes. But the core element of all professional learning is mentorship, as you will see in this section, and mentorship is the primary method of training tradespeople.

Universities provide both breadth and depth in their education. The breadth is the primary focus of the first couple of years of college. It goes by various names, but most universities refer to it as *general education*. The object of general education is to give students the kind of broad educational experiences that will make them well-rounded and flexible enough to adjust to changes in the economy. One reason most students are encouraged to take these courses in the first couple of years is that it is common for these experiences to awaken new avenues for a student to pursue. The depth dimension is the focus of chapter 6, in which we cover the process of selecting and completing both a college major and typically a college minor. These do not lock students into a single career, but they often determine where a student starts a career once the degree is completed.

It has often been said that it is not *what* you know that counts, but *who* you know. Although this claim is mostly false, it is not entirely false. What is clearly false is that it does matter what you know. The more you know and the better you know it, the more competitive you can be. But connections count, not so much for your success, but rather to help you to get a foot in the door. We will focus on how connections work, how to build the right connections, and how to use those connections in chapter 7.

College courses are an effective way of teaching material in a consistent and predictable manner, but students who only take courses will not learn all that is possible in college. A college or university attracts bright, motivated, and driven individuals, many of whom have gone on to change the world and many more who will change the world. Nothing shapes people's character and work style than the people around them. Anyone can sign up for a course with a skilled teacher, and they will learn things in that course. But to really learn about the field and what professionals do to excel in that field, you need to work more closely with faculty. Such opportunities are available, but those opportunities are competitive and may take considerable effort to obtain. Once you obtain them, maintaining them takes even more effort, but the effort is well worth the time and energy, as you will learn in chapter 8.

Many undergraduate degrees immediately open specific career opportunities. For example, people with degrees in education, business, and engineering often go directly into specific careers. That does not mean that they know everything they need to know in those field from four years of study. There will be more to learn, and they will learn it on the job in the next few years. Moreover, they will need to continue to learn because, if they stop learning, they will soon be outdated and incompetent.

Other careers use the undergraduate program to prepare you for advanced training that is far more specialized. This includes professional school (law and medicine, for example) and graduate programs in specific fields. These are demanding and competitive programs. It is not unusual for students to work eighty to one hundred hours a week in such programs. But in many cases, the single most difficult task is to get into these programs. Chapter 9 teaches you what these programs look for when selecting students and how you can maximize your chances of entering one of those programs.

What pulls this entire section together is your ultimate career choice. Although your career choice does not dictate all your academic decisions, it influences many of them. We finish this section in chapter 10 by discussing careers, how to select them, and how to use your choice of careers to guide optimal decision-making in college.

Chapter 7
Selecting Majors and Minors

There is no perfect major or minor, and most college students enter college with little understanding of the broad range of fields in which they may specialize. Besides providing a broad education, and therefore insights into the wide range of problems facing the world, a general education allows students to sample areas of study that may be new to them. The sampling often leads students to rethink their original major and focus their energy on a new major and new career opportunities. In this chapter, we will focus on the process of selecting a major and a minor in college. The selection of a major is, of course, central to your career planning, which is the primary focus of chapter 10.

Every university has obligations to its students. The obligations do not include being everything to everyone. However, once a university has made a commitment to a program, its obligation to students is to provide all necessary resources for the students to successfully complete the program. That means that departments that attract few majors may be phased out in time, at least in terms of providing a major. The department is likely to continue to exist, providing courses as a resource to students in other majors, long after the department no longer offers a major in the field. I bring this topic up because the number of college-age individuals is dropping, and many universities are being forced to cut programs. That should be part of your thinking in selecting a program, but I want you to know that it is highly unlikely that any program will be cut so quickly that current students will not have time to complete a declared major.

No department is required to teach every conceivable course in a field. In fact, even the largest universities are rarely able to accomplish this goal. But if the department offers a major, it is required to have all the critical courses needed to prepare its students for either a career or advanced training. There is general agreement in most fields about what constitutes adequate training. This is why the required courses and experiences in a college major are remarkably similar between various colleges and universities. It is helpful for a student to understand the logic of the curriculum in their college major. This information can often be obtained from published materials from the university or from the Internet, which can provide useful discussions of college majors and careers. Talking with upperclassmen or graduate students or faculty advisors can also be enormously helpful in planning your major.

Colleges and universities typically make the process of planning your college major easier by having a regular rotation of required and optional courses. Core courses are typically taught every semester, often with multiple sections. More advanced courses may only be taught every other semester, but typically departments try to be predictable with the times those courses are taught. For example, a particular course may only be taught in the fall, but it will be taught every fall. Courses that are not typically required may only be taught every other year. At most universities, it is easy to see this pattern by looking at past semesters. Moreover, universities typically plan courses out at least a full year in advance. They may not be able to tell you who is teaching the course or the time and location of the course, but most courses that are listed a year in advance will in fact be taught in the semester they have been scheduled. Academic advisors can be very helpful in this regard. They are often aware of such schedules and can warn you of potential scheduling problems if you share your longer-term course plans.

The Logic of a Major

Virtually every major in college has core courses that provide critical skills on which the entire major is based. These are often prerequisites for other courses. In the course catalog, universities list these courses as a part of the freshman or sophomore curriculum. The advanced courses typically specify which of these core courses are required before one can take the advanced course.

That is what prerequisite means; you must complete the prerequisite course before you are allowed to take the next course.

Most college majors represent a field that is so broad that it has subdisciplines within the field. If you go on to graduate school, you will likely specialize in one of the subdisciplines. As an undergraduate, you will typically be required to have at least some level of expertise in each of the subdisciplines. If the number of subdisciplines is large, you likely will be required to have experience in a set number of them. In many majors, that means taking at least one course in each subdiscipline, typically selected from a set of available courses.

A popular misconception, which we will cover in the section on graduate school, is that if you intend to specialize in a subdiscipline in graduate school, you should take as many of your undergraduate courses as possible in that subdiscipline. At the undergraduate level, the best preparation for graduate training is to be well-versed in the entire field and not just a narrow subset of the field.

Many disciplines require undergraduate training in related fields. This is usually clearly stated in the requirements for the major. For example, many disciplines require specific math skills, and the math courses that cover those skills are part of the requirement for the major. When we cover graduate school, we will talk about the ways to discover what is expected long before you make your application.

In some departments, the nature of the material is such that it must be covered in a carefully prescribed order. For those majors, planning is critical, but the major usually lays out the plan for students to avoid scheduling problems. In most disciplines, there will always be some core courses that are the prerequisite for later courses, but there will be flexibility in exactly when you take those later courses. That flexibility sounds nice, but it has a potential hazard. If there is flexibility about when you can take the courses, the department often feels less compelled to organize the courses so that they never conflict with your schedule. To avoid such conflicts, you will want to create a schedule for yourself that extends out two or three semesters, and you will want to check to see that the courses you need for your schedule are being taught and at a time that will fit your schedule.

College Majors and Careers

Often, your major and your career goals are inextricably linked. It is hard to be a chemist without being a chemistry major. It is hard to be an engineer without being an engineering major. In other cases, the link between the college major and one's intended career is weaker. Law students, for example, may major in political science, psychology, philosophy, or a half dozen other disciplines. There are also majors that provide a solid background for dozens of different career directions. If you want to be a clinical psychologist, you would almost certainly be a psychology major in college and then go on to earn a master's or PhD degree. However, psychology undergraduates often use their degrees to go into other fields. There are fields that involve the skills and values associated with psychology. The people who work in human resources typically value helping others and are skilled at listening to find out the needs of the people they serve. Some psychological skills, such as being able to read other people, are critical to almost every leader, regardless of the leader's field.

No one is surprised to learn that students with certain majors have little difficulty finding jobs immediately after graduating (Fogg, Harrington, Harrington, & Shatkin, 2012). Most engineering students have little difficulty finding jobs in today's economy, for example. However, even there, it depends on the economy. When I graduated from college, the economy happened to be so bad that most engineering students were taking part-time jobs because there were no engineering jobs. Since I had started out as an engineering major and had many friends who were engineering majors, I was well aware of the situation. The point is that you can do everything right and may be sidelined for a while, at least, by factors outside your control. It is not a failure on your part; it is just the luck of the draw.

Some college majors do not directly prepare you for specific jobs and therefore do not immediately have an open career path. However, research suggests that those majors without a direct career path often do well over the course of their career (Grobman & Ramsey, 2020). The general skills they learned in their major and their other studies, combined with what they learn after they graduate, position these individuals for leadership careers. Getting the initial job may be a harder sell, but once someone obtains a position, their advancement is typically dictated by their performance and not by their college degree. Moreover, even for people in degree programs that offer immediate high-paying jobs, their advancement into management positions is often based on developing new skills that were not part of their major. Finally, sometimes a nontraditional major can be advantageous. For example, a student with a Spanish major who completes all the premed courses may be looked on favorably by medical school admissions committees because there is a strong need for physicians fluent in Spanish.

You should not rely on your major alone to help you get the best possible job. A degree is only a baseline credential. In fact, even your major/minor combination should not be the only credential you offer a potential employer or graduate training program. Think in terms of skills. In almost every field, basic information in fields such as economics, computers, accounting, and communication dramatically increases the strength of your résumé. Couple such courses with a part-time job or volunteer work that demonstrates that you indeed have those skills, and it strengthens your résumé considerably.

The Logic of a Minor

The largest difference between a college and a trade school education is that the college education includes not only intensive training in one area, but also broad training in general and relatively intensive training in a second area. The relatively intensive training is your college minor. Universities differ on their minor requirements, and departments within the university may also differ. Some departments, for example, have so many requirements (both within the major and from other departments) that they elect to eliminate the minor requirement for their student majors. Although I have heard criticism of this approach, I think it is easy to look at the approach as being a distributed minor that strengthens the qualifications of their majors. Two examples of this approach are engineering programs and specialized education programs (such a math education). These programs often do not require a minor, but the collection of required courses gives students a broad education.

There are two philosophies about how to select a minor. The first philosophy is that minors should provide a second area of expertise that will make one more effective in one's primary field of study. For example, minoring in another language can enhance opportunities in almost any career by allowing the individual to be bilingual.

A second philosophy is that the minor fills in gaps in the skills for a career in the major field. For example, a biology major may choose to minor in chemistry because all biological functions are the result of chemical interactions. Our entire body is a chemical factory; in fact, every cell in our body is a chemical factory, and all behaviors and traits are the results of chemical processes. Biology majors with sophistication in chemistry, especially organic chemistry, are likely to have more opportunities in their field.

There is also a third philosophy, although it is not as popular as the first two, that the minor is either a way of indulging intellectual curiosity or insurance for a changing economic environment. The world is changing so quickly that many careers are cut short, not because the individual is not capable, but because the career opportunities have been replaced by other opportunities. In such a case, the minor may provide basic skills on which one could easily develop a second career track.

The freedom to choose a minor depends in part on your career path. If you want to apply to medical school, you will take a premed undergraduate program. The program lists the courses that are required by virtually every medical school. The major and the minor are not necessarily fixed, but the flexibility to meet both the premed requirements and the major and minor requirements and still graduate on time will probably limit your choices.

Planning for Flexibility

Many people start college with little information on which to select a major. Therefore, they select a major based on the limited information they do have and later discover there are other areas they find far more interesting and/or suited to their temperament and skills. Of course, the logical thing to do is to adjust your goals based on this new information. That means changing your major and perhaps your minor as well.

It is not uncommon to change one's major. The National Center for Education says 80 percent of college students change their major at least once. It is hard to select the right major for yourself when you have so little information about possible majors. For that reason, some universities do not even allow students to declare a major until their sophomore year. That gives the student a chance to take a course or two in their intended major and fulfill many of the general education requirements for their degree. It also gives the student a chance to try out other areas by taking selected courses in areas that may be of interest. This helps but does not solve the problem of making the right decision about your major.

Changing your major is not as earth shattering as it may feel at the time. It is certainly reasonable to change your major if you discover that your original selection was not a good fit for you. The earlier you make that decision, the easier it is to make the change without adding time (and tuition money) to your college career. But even if it takes an extra year and more tuition to complete a new major, it is better to come out prepared for a career that you will enjoy than to feel trapped in a career choice that is not for you.

Universities understand this problem and structure their curricula to deal with it. In the first year or two of undergraduate study, you should avoid focusing only on courses in your major. Instead, you want to emphasize the exploration that is part of the general education requirements. This accomplishes two goals. The first is that you explore areas that are probably new to you and may end up being areas that you want to pursue. The second is that all those credits will apply to your degree no matter what your major. Therefore, changing your major will have only a minor impact on your ability to graduate in four years. If you complete your general education requirements during your first two years, you will have the flexibility to complete most of your major and minor requirements in the last two years.

Complicating the strategy of focusing on general education courses in your first year is that many of the strongest students arrive at college with substantial college credit from CCP courses taken in high school. That is both an advantage and a disadvantage. Having completed the courses before ever arriving on campus means that the student can complete the degree faster, but it also pressures the student into selecting a major more quickly. But the principle that students are better off selecting a career direction that is fulfilling than focusing on finishing the degree in record time still applies. Getting out of college a year earlier is not much of a dividend if it means you will be frustrated with your career choice.

Although you can normally change your major and still graduate in four years, that may not always be the case. For example, some majors sequence courses, and because of the sequence, you can only take so many courses each semester in that major. If you switch into one of those majors, you may be spending extra time just to complete the required courses for the degree. Even if that were to happen, it is not the end of the world. You may need an extra semester or two to complete your degree, but if you use those semesters to take courses that prepare you to be more competitive in your field, that extra time may pay huge dividends.

I personally had three majors as an undergraduate. I started in chemical engineering, although I must admit that my only reason for going into that field is I knew a chemical engineer and liked how he described his work. I also loved chemistry in high school. I found I love the chemistry part of chemical engineering more than the engineering part, so I switched my major to chemistry. Then I fell in love with the field that became my career: psychology.

It is worth noting that I fell in love with psychology because of my introductory course in the field, and the instructor for that course was the worst college instructor I ever had. But psychology departments often require their introductory students to be involved in research as subjects. It is part of their learning, although frankly many students think it is little more than indentured servitude. I changed my major because the research in which I was a subject intrigued me. The researchers were required to give us feedback at the end of the study as part of our learning and to answer any questions we might have. Rarely did student subjects ever spend more time than was necessary, so questions were few and far between. However, I had questions—lots of questions. The students who were running the studies, usually graduate students working on advanced degrees, loved the fact that I was interested in their work. Two of them invited me to lunch so they could continue to answer my questions. I was hooked. Although I became a clinical psychologist, my primary interest right from the beginning was understanding human behavior by studying it in the lab.

The point of the story of how I ended up in psychology is that it is not always formal courses that influence our career directions. We should be open to all experiences that may tell us more about ourselves and about our interests. Moreover, we should seek out experiences, such as research, study abroad, service, leadership roles, and student organizations, that can give us important insights into our values and talents. I certainly would never have considered being a psychology major based on my introductory psychology instructor. He could put anyone to sleep, and judging from some of the students sitting around me, he managed to do that on a regular basis.

Chapter Summary

The choice of your college major and your college minor are often related to your intended career. If you would like a career in business or engineering, you would be well advised to major in business or engineering. Some college majors are more tightly linked to careers than others. It would be difficult to get a job in engineering without an engineering degree and the skills you learn as part of earning that degree. However, it is possible to go into business without a business degree. Nevertheless, depending on the business you are going into, a business degree may be very helpful.

Often students select their major without sufficient information to make the best possible selection. A major that sounds exciting to them at the age of eighteen may prove to be far less exciting as they finish their second year of college. Having the courage to change your major can prevent you from committing a large portion of your life to a career that is unsatisfying. The odds are good that the courses that you took for an aborted major will be valuable to you in whatever major you select and complete. So the time you invested in a major you elected not to complete will not have been wasted.

Most college students must take general education courses as part of their degree requirements, and those courses can be an excellent way to learn about alternative areas of study for either your major or your minor. You want to consider those courses carefully so they can introduce you to areas that may capture your attention and your passion.

Chapter 8
Getting to Know the Right People

Some of you may find the title of this chapter offensive. It seems to imply that the way to get ahead is to use your connections. Whether you find that idea offensive or not, there is some truth to it. But the truth is not in having people do things for you or give you opportunities you do not deserve. The truth is that there will always be people who know what you need to know and whose job it is to help you solve the problems you face. Identifying these people and building appropriate relationships with them can help you tremendously in your undergraduate career and your entire professional career.

Who are these people, how do you find them, and how do you build relationships with them? These are the questions that are addressed in this chapter. In an era in which you address several questions a day to Google or Siri, it may seem irrelevant to think in terms of knowing the right people. Hardly a day goes by when I do not use a search engine to find the information I need. Having the skills to find such information through search engines, the library, and other data sources will be an extremely valuable part of the professional skills of the future. However, the type of information they provide tends to be factual. Finding the information that is most relevant for you in planning your college career still requires the help of knowledgeable individuals or the patient reading of a ton of material, only a small portion of which is likely to be personally relevant.

Google was not the first search engine. But once Google was introduced, it quickly became the dominant search engine. Why? Google did something that the other search engines did not do or did not do nearly as well: organized the information using a remarkably simple algorithm that was likely to present the most relevant information first. But relevance is relative; what is relevant for me may not be relevant for you. Using human consultants who possess a wide range of knowledge and skills is still the most effective way to answer many questions and give personal advice. But do not overlook casual exchanges with other like-minded people. They may not be as informed as consultants, but they usually know you well and may have just the right information for you.

This chapter discusses who is likely to have the wide range of knowledge you need for advice. You will learn that they are not always the people with the most impressive titles. The CEO of a company may be incredibly knowledgeable about the company and its goals but know next to nothing about a particular operation within the company. In an academic institution, the department chair may be able to answer questions about specific courses and career options, but often the administrative assistant for the department can give you more effective information about how to add a course, change a grade, or change your minor.

Advisors

Universities know that students often arrive with more questions than information. Students need information on everything from which courses to take to how to explore new areas. Most universities have formal advisement programs that range from having a professional available to answer student questions to having regular advisement meetings with a faculty member.

The best advisors are likely to give you information and principles for making decisions instead of just telling you what to do. They may, for example, point out that the general education requirements are a great way to explore areas that may end up being your major or your minor. They may also tell you how you can plan your program to finish required courses on time and not have to extend your undergraduate career. If your advisor does not give you principles you can follow, you should take steps to learn those principles. There are two ways to do this. First, simply ask for principles, such as, "What should I be focusing on in each of my four years of college?" The second is to determine what the principles seem to be and ask the advisor if your determination is accurate. For example, you may note that the advisor seems to be emphasizing general education courses rather than major courses. You can then ask your advisor whether it is advisable to focus on the general education courses rather than make a huge initial commitment to a specific major. Again, the best advisors will likely share these principles with you, but not all advisors are "the best." A principle here is that you want to learn to advocate for yourself. If you are not getting the information and help you need, it is perfectly reasonable to seek help elsewhere.

Resource Programs

If you are disciplined enough, you can learn almost anything by reading. Few of us are that disciplined. We learn better by learning together. We learn better when we have specific assignments. We learn better when we have deadlines to meet. Universities facilitate this by creating courses and putting those courses into fixed periods of time (quarters or semesters).

But not everything has to be done within a semester schedule or even through courses. Most universities have informal programs that are almost always free. They may include clubs or organizations in which students with similar interests get together to explore those interests. They may include honor societies in which strong students with specific interests learn together. They can also be programs designed to help students develop specific skills. For example, almost every student can benefit from having their writing critiqued by a good writer. Most universities have writing programs that offer such critiques. Those writing programs usually have students who write well help other students to identify ways they can improve their writing. I always encourage my students to use such services. If you want to be a better writer, you must write often, and you must have good writers review your work with a critical eye.

These resource programs at the university are a great place to start if you want to improve your understanding and skills. For example, joining the physics club if you are a physics major will help you learn more about the field and the direction it is going. Using a writing program on campus can certainly help you improve the quality of your own writing. However, if you really want to succeed, you need to recognize that the natural progression is to move from being a consumer to being a producer. For example, at some point you may become an officer in the physics club and may coordinate programs designed to help younger physics majors understand the field. If you become an excellent writer, you may be selected as one of those students in the university's writing center that helps other students improve their writing.

The best way to understand any area is to focus your learning so you can be more effective in teaching. The process of teaching others allows you to see how well you understand what you are teaching. You often learn more as part of the process of teaching others than you learn in the classes you took on the topic. We cannot teach something we do not understand, but students often do not realize they do not understand something until they imagine themselves teaching it to someone else. The teaching need not be formal; simply filling in other students on the material covered when they missed a class often highlights the areas we still do not understand well. People do not have to be perfect to be teachers; if we did, there would be no teachers for us to learn from. Teachers are still learning, and they often learn what they need to learn by realizing they do not know it well enough to teach it effectively.

People Who Know How to Get Things Done

Titles are nice because they give us an idea of what we can expect from people. We expect that college professors (a title) know the material in their area of expertise well enough to be able to teach it or conduct research on it. We expect advisors to know the rules well enough to be able to answer questions and give us useful information. We expect handymen (or handywomen) to be able to fix things around the house. But titles are not the only way to determine what people know.

Every organization has a few people behind the scenes who are amazingly good at getting things done. They may not have the official title, but their record of achievement suggests they can solve problems. For example, the department chair may know a lot about the field, the faculty, and general university procedures.

However, the department assistant is more likely to know how to submit a change of grade form or what office handles a particular procedure.

One of the most impressive people I have ever met was the chief of psychology at the VA hospital in Buffalo, New York. Her name was Elenore (Ellie) Jacobs. She was the very first person to earn a PhD in clinical psychology from the department I taught in for nearly twenty-five years. To put that into perspective, most undergraduates at the time were male, and it was rare for females to be in any graduate program, much less be the first to graduate from the program. She was a superstar in every sense of the word. She was not only the chief of her service but also probably the most respected chief of service in the entire hospital. Her work elevated the entire psychology service in the eyes of the professionals in the hospital, although the fact that she had a great eye for talent and tended to hire incredibly competent people certainly helped. I served on committees with her for more than twenty years and learned so much from her.

Ellie solidified in my mind a principle that I had begun to appreciate before I met her. The principal is simple: usually the person with the title approves an action, but that person is almost never the person who can get the action done. Often after you get approval, you turn to the person's assistant to get the job done. (By the way, the assistants at the time usually had the title of *secretary*, which certainly did not capture all the skills and talent they brought to the job.) You need to treat those individuals well. It takes little effort to treat someone well. Express legitimate gratitude for the things they do for you; praise them for the skills they use to solve your problems; take time to chat with them and get to know them. In other words, treat them the way they deserve to be treated. I have always been amazed at the stupidity of some professionals who treat such individuals with disrespect. Besides being obnoxious, such behavior is professional suicide in that these people are often critical to one's professional success.

As a student, you may be thinking that developing relationships with key people in the university is impossible. It is not, and the effort it takes to build those relationships is not only personally rewarding, but also can save your butt if or when things go wrong. Something as small as showing appreciation when they help you with one of the paperwork tasks that are part of the university can go a long way. Demonstrating that you understand how much they know by asking their advice on how to solve a problem is powerful. Most students just ask to meet with the chair, as if the chair's assistant knows nothing about how to solve problems. If the person is not too busy to chat and seems interested in chatting, take time and talk. When you are done, tell them that you enjoyed the conversation and that you appreciate all the person does for you and the other students. The next time you ask a question, I guarantee you will get the best possible response.

Finally, a word of advice. It is good form to meet the right people before you need their help. It is easier to stop by during an instructor's office hours to say how much you are enjoying the course and perhaps ask for suggestions on what you may read beyond the course material than to stop by only after you do poorly on the first exam. The instructor will still help you understand how to do better on the exams if it is your first visit, but you can expect the instructor to be motivated to help if your prior contacts have been around your excitement rather than a poor grade.

People Who Know People

The assistants described in the previous section are often the people who get things done, but they have another secret weapon: when they do not know how to do something themselves, they are usually part of a network of talented behind-the-scenes individuals who can get almost anything done.

Universities have begun to realize that they need to compete for students, and this is a great thing. Why? Because it is in the interests of the university to make life for students as easy as possible, or at least a lot less frustrating. They do this by creating offices that break through the bureaucracy and find the information and the people students need to solve their individual issues. Most universities now have such programs, and the few that do not have made efforts to steer students in the right direction in other ways. Find out if such a program exists, and if so, put its location, phone number, and email address into your phone. That way, you have a place to go to answer most of the questions you will face as a student.

Transitional People

When you start college, advisors and other knowledgeable people will be among the most important people in your life. They will help you find the information and make the choices that will make your college life run smoothly. But the point of college is not to go to college. The point of college is to prepare you for the real world. So there will be a time during your college career when most of your energy will be focused on what you will do after college. Some advisors move smoothly from helping you navigate college to preparing you to be more competitive for jobs and graduate training, but that is not true of all advisors. You will need to identify those individuals who can help you transition to the next stage.

Most students understand they will need the advice of such people, but few students realize they should be getting that advice early. If you do not start to think about what you will do after you graduate until your senior year, it is much too late to be highly competitive. Graduate applications are due early in your senior year, and for those applications to be competitive, you need to have made the right choices to stand out from the other candidates.

My best advice is to have tentative ideas of what you want to do after graduation early in your sophomore year, and if you have an advisor, share those plans with him or her and ask for his or her advice. Also join professional organizations on campus. Many departments will have clubs or honor societies in their field, and the advisors for these groups often help students increase their competitiveness for jobs and graduate training. Moreover, many of the students in these groups intend to go into a professional field and have been searching for information on how to be more competitive. What they have learned can easily be shared with you, and in time, you will be sharing that same information with other students.

Everyone Else

Unlike books, people do not come with an index. You cannot tell by looking at them what their life has been like, what they know, what they are particularly good at, and who they may know. But if you take the time to get to know them, you may be surprised at how many people you already know could be enormously helpful resource people for you.

We all learn how to meet new people and get to know them. Some people are more comfortable doing this than others, and some people truly enjoy getting to know people who once were strangers. But getting to know people is a challenge, and it is a challenge with potential hazards. When we first meet someone, we tend to stick with safe topics, such as the weather or activities you know the person enjoys. We tend to avoid potential conversational landmines, such as politics, religion, or personal philosophy. That is fine when we first meet someone, but if we rarely talk about anything other than the weather, we will never get to know that person.

When I was younger, I was amazed at the people who could easily talk with others. I was not particularly outgoing, so I looked up to those who seemed more outgoing. It seemed to me that they knew so much and were so interesting that people wanted to talk with them. Frankly, I was naïve. On closer analysis, I discovered that most of those people who were such good conversationalists did far more listening than talking. They often asked great questions that helped open the conversation to new topics. In the process, those individuals got to know an incredible array of things, which they later shared with others. They also got to know what things their new friends could do that they had no idea how to do. You may learn from a casual conversation that one of your friends loves golf and is familiar with locations for golf vacations. Alternatively, you may have another friend that is a great cook, who can tell you the best way to learn specific cooking skills. However, you must get beyond the topic of weather to learn these things, and you must develop the skill of asking the right questions and encouraging your friends to open up by listening carefully to what they say.

People like to talk about themselves, especially if the person they are talking to is interested. It is not hard to be interested in other people. However, unless you are a sociopath, it is hard to fake interest in other people. You will not always have time to chat with people and get to know them. But when you do have the time to get to know people, you will soon find such conversations enjoyable and rewarding. You may also be surprised at how positively people judge you when you spend time listening to them and asking them questions.

The more people you know and the more you know about them, the more likely you will know someone who can give you great advice when you need it. Those same people are also likely to be able to write strong letters of recommendation when you need them.

There are many products I would not consider buying without talking with a knowledgeable friend, and I know they are knowledgeable because of casual conversations I have had with them. Some of my friends have incredible knowledge about areas that I know next to nothing about. I may never need to know that information, but if life circumstances put me in a position where I need that information, I know where to go. When people say, "It is not what you know but who you know," they are leaving out an important element. That element is that who you know is only valuable if you also know what each of those people knows and which of those people could help in your situation. If you have not bothered to get to know people, you will never know when they could be an important resource.

Symbiotic Relationships

Every stable relationship is symbiotic, even those that do not appear to be on the surface. In symbiotic relationships, both parties benefit, although not always at the same time. If you fall in love, you benefit because you both enjoy the overwhelming positive feelings when you are together. In traditional friendships, you both benefit from the enjoyable times you spend together and from the times you help one another. It is rare that you both need help at the same time, but if you can count on the other person for help, you still feel the symbiotic nature of the relationship. If, however, you constantly wanted things from your friend and were unwilling to reciprocate when your friend needed help, the relationship would not last. You may think that a newborn could not possibly live up to the demands of a symbiotic relationship but hold one for a few minutes and you will quickly see that nature gave that newborn the ability to melt your heart with just a glance or a smile.

In the professional relationships we are talking about in this book, keeping the relationships symbiotic is especially important. Many of the people you will deal with in college and in your continued education are being paid to provide services, but providing quality service or mentorship is hard work. Expressing your gratitude on a regular basis goes a long way toward fulfilling that symbiotic contract. The more intense the relationship, the more opportunity you will have to contribute to the relationship. If a mentor is your boss or the head of the lab in which you are doing a thesis, doing the very best job you can to make your boss or mentor proud will nurture a long-term relationship.

Relationships are naturally multidimensional, and they change over time. They also have limitations. For example, professors may have excellent connections (i.e., relationships) with their students in class, but they are expected not to have romantic relationships because of the obvious power imbalance. Similar rules are in place in corporations. But mentorship relationships can develop into friendships, and those friendships may last long after the mentorship relationship is no longer present. As those changes occur, the expectations for the symbiotic relationship change, but the importance of symbiosis never disappears.

Chapter Summary

Although talent, hard work, and passion will always be important to success, having the right contacts can be a useful adjunct strategy. Traditionally, we think of knowing the right people as knowing powerful people, and sometimes that is true. But often, the people who can be most helpful to us when we need it are ordinary people in ordinary positions, although you may well discover that some of these people are extraordinary. These people can often run interference, point us in the right direction when we need help, or make a single phone call that can help resolve an issue. They do not expect to be paid; they only hope that we will appreciate their efforts on our behalf.

You will meet many people in college, and some of them will be critical to your future success. Some people are naturally comfortable meeting new people; others are less comfortable with meeting others. If you are in that latter category, do not give up hope. Meeting new people is just a skill. You introduce yourself, explain your situation, and respond positively to the other person. This quick introduction is often referred to as the elevator pitch (what you can communicate in a short elevator ride). Granted, some introductions may be easier than others. For example, it may be easy to introduce yourself to the administrative assistant in your department who will handle the paperwork for getting you into the class because that person is often tasked with helping students. It may be harder to introduce yourself to someone you find attractive in a bar. There is more risk in the bar because people in bars are not being paid to help you out. You may never be comfortable picking up someone in a bar; I never was. But with practice, you can become effective at meeting and interacting with people within a professional context, and college is a great place to learn how to interact with such people.

It is easy to justify treating people well on moral grounds alone. But such behavior also has the advantage of building goodwill in individuals who may or may not do us a favor in the future. Many of those people are professional enough that they will do us a favor even if we have not treated them well, but they are more likely to do us a favor if they feel appreciated by us, and they are more likely to do it quickly and happily. The best leaders routinely treat other people fairly, and in the process, they often experience loyalty from those people.

Chapter 9
Intensive Study Opportunities

T he unit of study at universities is the course. Departments and majors develop integrated programs that are defined by a specific set of courses. Much of what you learn in college will be learned in courses. In fact, most students get almost all their learning in college from courses. But if you are interested in excelling in your field, I recommend that you look for other more intensive and individualized experiences.

At many universities, each department will have a course with a title like Independent Study. Once, independent study was common. If a student wanted to learn about things that were not covered in a course and there was a faculty member who wanted to teach that material or learn it together with the student, they would contract to have the student study the material on their own and meet individually with the faculty member.

Such an arrangement is almost never found in the modern university. Faculty are simply too busy to give that level of individual attention to students. However, there are variations on this theme that are well worth exploring. I will cover four such options in this section. The first is an advanced seminar course, which is typically on a narrow topic of interest of the faculty member and usually has a small class size. The second is working with faculty members on their research or other professional work. The third is volunteer activity either at the university or in a related setting that gives you specific experiences. Finally, the fourth is a job that utilizes the skills you learned as a student and has you apply those skills in a professional setting.

These experiences have several advantages. The first is that they offer the opportunity to get a much deeper level of understanding of your area of specialization. They also look good on a job application or an application for graduate or professional school because they typically represent a credential that is only possible if you are an exceptionally strong student. The third is that they give you an opportunity to get to know a faculty member much better than you could ever get to know that faculty member in a classroom. More importantly, the faculty member will get to know you and therefore will be in a much better position to write you a strong letter of recommendation. Of course, how strong the letter is will depend on how good you performed in your work with that faculty member or supervisor. A fourth advantage is that such experience can give you information about career paths you had never considered or, alternatively, convince you that the career path you thought you wanted is not actually right for you. In the latter case, it is much better to learn that now than years later.

Senior Seminars

No one will be surprised to hear that college is expensive. Many universities deal with the high cost by making classes larger or using graduate students or adjunct faculty to teach many of the courses. Most universities try to have occasional courses, typically at the junior and senior levels, that are more narrowly focused, have smaller class sizes, and are a much more intimate setting to cover the material and get to know the faculty members. Faculty often love teaching these courses because typically they are on a topic that is near and dear to the faculty member. Many students shy away from such courses because they tend to be more intense and demanding than traditional courses. For that reason, they can be an ideal experience that will serve a serious student well.

These courses are much closer to a graduate-level course than an undergraduate course. They are more likely to cover original research rather than summarize the field. Such courses dramatically improve the critical thinking of students because of the nature of the content and the intensity of the interaction between faculty and students. When a faculty member teaches fifty students or five hundred students, there is little opportunity to get to know the students. In a small intense course, like the one described here, the faculty member will usually get to know the students, although even here, students must prove themselves by actively participating. At the very least, if you do well in the course, it will lead to a strong letter of recommendation.

All recommendation letters start out with a paragraph that describes how one knows the person. A good letter from someone who says that you were in a couple of their courses and got an A will be helpful. However, the same good letter from someone who has worked with you intensely in a small seminar course will carry more weight. The faculty member will have more information about you from a small seminar course and can comment on your ability to think on your feet, communicate, and analyze difficult questions.

Sometimes, such small courses can lead to connections that may be even more valuable to your long-term career. Faculty who are interested in getting the best possible people to be a part of their research lab (see next section) will often actively recruit the best people from small and intense courses like this.

Research Lab Teams

In many university departments, the single most common and best way to get invaluable experience that will make you more competitive on the job market and for graduate programs is to work with faculty members in their lab. All faculty members at virtually every university are supposed to be scholars, and most indeed are scholars. They not only teach material but also conduct research that enhances our knowledge and may be part of courses in the future. They do their research in conjunction with their students, which could include both graduate and undergraduate students.

The way this works depends entirely on the university. At some universities, you can earn credit for such research; at other universities, there is no course credit involved. In the latter case, there will be nothing on your transcript about this work, but then again, there also is no charge on your tuition bill. It may even be possible to get a paid research position. That is the best of all possible situations because you not only get great experience but also make some money at the same time.

What makes these relationships so valuable is that they are symbiotic. Students get an opportunity to learn things that could not possibly be learned from a textbook, and they also benefit from the fact that the instructor gets to know them well enough to write strong letters of recommendation. The faculty member benefits because the presence of bright and highly motivated students stimulates their thinking and facilitates their work. Depending on the nature of the lab, students that get involved may contribute enough to a project that they may qualify as a coauthor on a conference presentation or publication. Finally, students who work in a lab starting early enough in their undergraduate career may well become experts in the field, and this could lead to an agreement with the faculty member to sponsor a senior thesis or honors thesis. Because the student knows the area well from their prior lab work, their research studies are likely to be more sophisticated and therefore more publishable. Being a coauthor on a research study, or even the senior author if it is primarily your own research, will dramatically improve your competitiveness for graduate training and beyond.

Many students believe that the research experience they get as an undergraduate should be in the area they intend to study as a graduate student. That would be nice, but it is not necessary. An advantage of working with someone in the field you would like to pursue is that that professor is likely to know faculty in the field at other universities. Consequently, they can be a great source of information. More importantly, if they write you a letter of recommendation and the people reading their letter know them and their work, the letter of recommendation will carry more weight. Think of it this way: a professional's reputation rests on whether other professionals trust them. That is certainly true of their research, but it is also true of their letters of recommendation. Professionals are reluctant to write letters of recommendation that say you can walk on water when they know that some of the people reading those letters will be upset if they discover they were lying. That is why someone well known in the field is unlikely to write a strong letter that is not backed up by data. Therefore, when they do write a strong letter, it is taken seriously.

If you can work in a lab of a productive faculty member in an area different from what you would like to ultimately study, work with that faculty member. The skills you learn from such work easily carry over into other fields of study. Moreover, researchers routinely borrow ideas from various subfields of their discipline. Learning about one or more of those subfields will give you insights that may well help you later in your career.

It is a common misconception among students that most of their undergraduate education should be focused on the narrow area that they want to study in graduate school. That is simply not true, and the strongest evidence for that is that most graduate programs require a broad base of study. The reason for that broad base is that professionals are more effective with such a broad understanding of the field and related fields.

Volunteer Activity

Skills make people more competitive for jobs or graduate training. The best professionals have a wide range of skills, and they pick up those skills in a wide variety of ways. One of the most overlooked ways is volunteer activity. The activity may be on campus, such as writing for the school newspaper, or it may be off campus, such as tutoring high school students on a volunteer basis.

Volunteer activity always looks good on your résumé, but the skills learned through volunteer activity look even better on your résumé. Most volunteer agencies need people at many different levels and often have activities that require little or no training. Those activities are important, and if you help with them, you have a right to feel good about your work. But some volunteer agencies also have more demanding tasks that would be an opportunity to learn skills and/or to demonstrate those skills. They may include such things as putting together a newsletter, coordinating social media efforts, building a database to help manage their services, or training new people for specific positions. Look for those opportunities and volunteer if you have the time and the interest. Besides giving you skills that may serve you well in the future, such behavior will almost certainly justify a strong letter of recommendation when it comes time to apply for jobs or for graduate or professional training.

Work Experience

It is a fact of life that many students cannot afford college without the income from a part-time job. Even with part-time work, students may need to take out loans, but at least the income from the work reduces the size of the loans. Working part time as a student clearly takes away some of the time that you could devote to studying. However, it is not realistically possible to study twelve hours a day. So a reasonable level of part-time work can easily fit into a college schedule. In fact, research shows that part-time work does not negatively affect academic performance provided it does not exceed twenty hours a week. The question of what kind of work would be most beneficial can and should be addressed when selecting potential jobs.

What jobs are available to college students will depend on many factors, the most important being the job market. As I write this, the job market is great, with high salaries and flexibility in scheduling, and some jobs even come with signing bonuses. But in my lifetime, there have been times when you had to walk on water to be able to get any job. For the sake of this discussion, I am going to assume that we have a reasonable job market with options available.

For most students, the two most important criteria for a job are salary and flexibility. On-campus jobs often have the most flexibility, but they may not always be available. Jobs that require you to be there when you should be in class are not a good idea. Jobs that pay better will help with the tuition and leave you little extra for having fun with friends. There is nothing wrong with either of those criteria. But it would be nice to add some other criteria that would make the job more useful to your long-term career aspirations. Depending on your major and where you are in your college career, you likely have skills that would qualify you for more demanding work. For example, I was able to get a job in the engineering department as an undergraduate because I had one year of chemistry, and they needed someone who could prepare the chemicals for an engineering laboratory course. You may have skills with computer programs, with working with people, or in writing reports. Those jobs not only will be more useful to you but are also likely to pay better.

Even if you take a traditional job, such as working in the fast-food industry, there are things you can do that will make that job more valuable. For example, when you interview, ask about the opportunities for advancement into leadership positions. That is a great way to tell people that you are ambitious, hardworking, and enjoy responsible positions. If you follow through after being hired, the line on your résumé for that job will be far more impressive than it would be otherwise. Instead of saying that you worked at a McDonald's, for example, you can say that you worked at McDonald's and within six months was a shift supervisor. Trust me, that is not a subtle difference, and people will notice. One does not get promoted to a management position without proving him or herself, and if you look at the histories of highly successful people, they have consistently shown this kind of leadership and advancement in everything they did.

You can also enhance the benefits of a part-time job by thinking in terms of the skills that you can develop and refine. For example, most jobs demand communication and collaboration skills. Identify how those skills are important, reflect on how you may improve those skills, and imagine how you can use those skills in your career. These steps will impress your boss while also adding important elements to your résumé. Recognize that earning the right to take on additional responsibilities represents an opportunity. Things like opening and closing, handling money, or dealing with customers will build your skill set and pay huge dividends in the future. Every professional career involves proving that you are responsible, capable, and dedicated to solving problems for people. Why not get in the habit of behaving that way early?

The time restrictions associated with being a college student will always limit your work opportunities, but an amazing number of employers are willing to work with their best people so they can keep great employees. Make sure you are one of those "best people." Express your appreciation for whatever accommodations the employer is willing and able to make so you can continue your college career. Such behavior is simply good manners, but it is often the difference between having a great job that pays well and provides security throughout college and constantly looking for other jobs.

Chapter Summary

The structure of universities often suggests that virtually all learning occurs in classrooms. Some learning clearly does occur in classrooms, but it is possible to develop critical skills outside the classroom. If you want to be a successful college student, go on to higher education, and be a successful professional, you will want to take advantage of all available opportunities. I strongly encourage students to use the classroom experience to learn as much as they can, but at the same time I want to acknowledge that the vast majority of what you will learn in your lifetime will not be learned in classrooms. By the time you are in college, you want to take control of your learning outside of the classroom.

Learning through work in a faculty member's laboratory, volunteer activities, or a part-time job is a valuable addition to your résumé. Not only can you develop skills that you are unlikely to develop in a classroom, but also you can prove yourself by being able to point to specific achievements. I would be lying if I said that grades did not count, but everyone who selects people for jobs and graduate programs knows that being able to get good grades is not enough. Having things on your résumé that show that you are dependable, able to balance a challenging schedule, and able to learn new skills and take leadership roles will dramatically strengthen any application you may make.

Chapter 10
Planning for Graduate or Professional School

S tudents often realize early in their undergraduate career that their career goals will require additional education beyond the undergraduate degree. However, students often incorrectly assume that decisions on postgraduate studies can be put off until their senior year. Nothing could be further from the truth. The preparation for successfully applying to graduate or professional school takes well more than a year. Moreover, the application deadline for many graduate and professional programs is as early as the first semester of your senior year.

Although it may be technically possible to do everything necessary to apply to graduate school starting in September of your senior year, it would be a foolish mistake to do so. There are so many things that you can do to enhance your application starting in your sophomore year. In this chapter, I will cover the things you can do to be competitive for these advanced training programs. I will focus primarily on graduate school, especially PhD programs, but I will also cover master's programs and applications to program such as law school, medical school, and MBA programs.

There is one principle that applies to all post-graduate education programs. If you wait until your senior year to apply, you likely will have missed opportunities to strengthen your application, and therefore, you may have difficulty getting into the program you want.

PhD Programs

Virtually every field has a graduate-level degree associated with it. Typically, the highest degree you can earn in a field is a PhD, or Doctor of Philosophy. Compare it to the MD degree, or Doctor of Medicine; or the EdD, or Doctor of Education. You may wonder why fields as diverse as chemistry, history, engineering, and psychology all share the same degree. Historically, any advanced-study program involved the generic study of basic principles, which was referred to as *philosophy*. If the graduate program was in the sciences, the advanced study was often referred to as *natural philosophy* (i.e., the study of nature). By convention, virtually all advanced degrees were thought to be philosophy degrees with an area of specialization. So, the degree is PhD (Doctor of Philosophy) in, for example, theoretical physics (the area of specialization).

Specialization

Specialization is a necessary evil in the complex professional world we live in. To be an expert in any field, you must devote much of your study to that field. However, experts typically are required to know about other related fields. This breath requirement positions an expert to be successful.

Many of the modern fields of study were part of other fields originally. Chemistry, for example, is an outgrowth of physics, and physics is an outgrowth of natural philosophy. Even within a field, there are subfields. For example, chemistry is often broken down into quantitative, organic, and physical chemistry. Psychology is often broken down into developmental, social, cognitive, physiological, and clinical psychology. Furthermore, within psychology, there are often narrower applied programs, such as industrial/organizational psychology, forensic psychology, or school psychology.

Undergraduate training in every field requires that you learn each of the subfields, and graduate training requires an even higher level of knowledge in the subfields. So, for example, students planning on grad school in clinical psychology should not try to take all their undergraduate courses in clinical psychology. In fact, the undergraduate programs will require that they take courses across a broad range of psychology. In addition, when students reach the graduate level, they will be required to learn even more about these nonclinical subdisciplines.

The rationale for this requirement is simple. Psychology is the broad overarching discipline, and the subdisciplines within psychology share much in common. They use the same methods for understanding and studying phenomena, and they often build on the ideas and principles of other subdisciplines in the field. Clinical psychology borrows heavily from all fields of psychology to address the applied question of diagnosing and treating various kinds of psychological disorders. To work with clients, you must know how they will respond to social demands; how their developmental history will shape their personality and typical responses to difficult situations; how they think, remember, and perceive the world around them; and how their physiology creates the biological substrate for all these phenomena. To be a clinical psychologist, you must first be a psychologist who understands all these subtleties.

The above example of how a discipline and its subdisciplines are related focuses on psychology, but the principles apply to virtually every discipline. University disciplines that are advanced enough to have a formal department and to offer a PhD almost always have subdisciplines, and most departments that have subdisciplines will offer a specific PhD in each of those subdisciplines.

Many fields of study are dependent on other fields, and so many undergraduate programs have required courses that are outside of a student's major. For example, many biology programs require basic chemistry or organic chemistry because these fields are critical in understanding the core concepts of biology. Mathematics is so critical to many fields that mathematics courses are routine requirements for those majors. If you major in those fields, you likely will be required to take courses in calculus or differential equations. These undergraduate requirements will be clearly spelled out in course catalogs, and they are strictly enforced for you to be granted your degree in that major.

Some graduate programs require such diverse backgrounds that they routinely provide guidance to students. Medical schools are a good example; they require a standard curriculum referred to as a *premed course of study*. The student can select from several majors, but if the student wants to apply to medical school, he or she will need to complete all the premed required courses as part of the application package.

Unfortunately, few graduate programs provide this level of guidance. However, most faculty in a program are familiar with graduate programs because those faculty earned a graduate degree in the field. It is wise for students to take advantage of the expertise of faculty by letting them know their interest in graduate or professional training. Depending on the university, students may or may not have a faculty advisor, but all universities provide some source of advisement for students. It can also be helpful to seek advice from graduate or professional programs you are interested in attending. These programs are often willing to suggest courses or experiences that will better prepare you for advanced study in their department.

Being More Competitive

Most PhD programs are focused on the training of people who will spend most of their professional life advancing the discipline. What that means is that those who earn their PhD will do research in the field and teach students about the field. You want to put together an application package that indicates (1) that you understand and want that career and (2) that you have focused on building the skills in college to prepare you for graduate school and a career in scholarship.

The application package typically involves three elements: your scores, your personal statement, and letters of recommendation. They are all important, but in different ways. As we cover this package, it is important for you to realize the nature of the evaluation process. Unlike college applications, which are usually handled by an office of recruitment professionals, your graduate applications are reviewed by the faculty who provide your graduate training. These people are busy with their teaching, their mentoring of graduate students, and their scholarship (research and publications). Applications typically come in near the end of the first semester. The applications are usually not available for review until nearly Christmas, and the second semester starts about two or three weeks after Christmas. It is common to have dozens of applications, and some programs routinely get hundreds of applications. With so many applications to review in a short time, you want your application to stand out immediately in that pool.

Your Scores

Students often focus too heavily on the scores, which include your GPA and scores on tests like the Graduate Record Exam (GRE). Generally, most schools do not make selections for graduate school based on scores. Instead, the scores provide a minimum criterion for considering the application. When a school publishes minimum GRE scores and GPAs, it is best to take them seriously. In most cases, published minimums are indeed taken seriously by the program, and your application will not be reviewed if you do not meet those minimum scores. These universities typically have far more candidates than they can accept, and sometimes they have far more candidates than they can even evaluate. From their perspective, they know that they can get more than enough great students from a smaller pool and therefore do not need to review every possible candidate. They realize that there are likely to be some great students they are overlooking because their scores are below those minimums, but they have accepted that cost in exchange for looking more closely at a smaller group of clearly strong candidates.

Your GPA will already be in place by the time you complete your applications to graduate school. In general, your GPA for your freshman and sophomore years is a less effective predictor of graduate school success than your junior/senior GPA. Occasionally, a school will ask you to compute those two GPAs, but even if they do not, you can bring it to their attention in your statement. Perhaps you needed time to get focused when you first started college; perhaps your initial major did not arouse your passion. If your GPA improved dramatically as you continued college, point that out. If there are other aspects of your academic record, those can also be covered in your statement. However, it is best to use your personal statement to emphasize the positive and avoid giving too many excuses for lower grades.

You want to do well on the GRE, and the best way to do that is to give yourself time to prepare. The GRE includes three subtests: verbal reasoning, mathematical reasoning, and analytical writing. There are excellent preparation courses, but they are expensive. You can generally get more bang for the buck by purchasing one or more GRE study guides and diligently setting aside time every week for preparing. In fact, you may not even have to spend your money because many universities make these study guides available free through the library or other student resource center. There are also GRE subject tests in selected content areas (chemistry, mathematics, physics, and psychology). Some graduate programs require these tests, but many do not. Graduate programs typically make it clear on their website whether such subject tests are expected.

If your field of study does not use mathematics routinely, you can benefit dramatically by refreshing your knowledge of high school mathematics. You can also benefit from learning how the sections of the GREs work so you have a strategy for attacking each of those sections. Trying to memorize lists of words is not generally worth the effort. That is not how we expand our vocabulary. The fact that the GRE includes an analytical writing subtest is an indication of how important it is for you to work to master your writing skills in college. The single most important thing you can do to prepare for the GRE is to make sure you are well-rested and relaxed when you take the exam. It is hard to be relaxed if you are taking the exam at the last minute when you are likely overwhelmed by the demands of your senior year and the work associated with applying for graduate school. Therefore, you want to start working on the application process early so such stress is not a part of the process for you.

Your Personal Statement

The personal statement is the most important part of your application and the part you have the greatest control over. It also will be one of the most difficult things you ever write. You want the statement to sell your application; you do not want the statement to give the wrong message. The message you want to present is that you are a sophisticated student who knows what graduate school involves and has systematically prepared yourself for graduate school. You want a tight, effective statement, with your claims about your readiness clearly backed up with data. Do not start with an account of something that happened when you were ten years old, especially if it is a long story. You will lose the reader by the end of the second paragraph if your statement does not focus on why you should be considered for graduate school. Because of the importance of this statement, it would be a great idea to ask your advisor or other faculty members to read it and offer suggestions.

Your statement should be short, focused, and supported by data. If the program suggests a maximum length, do not go beyond their suggestion. You want the faculty member reading the statement to know by the end of the first paragraph that you understand what is expected in graduate school and that you are prepared. Think of every paragraph after the first one as having a hypothetical topic sentence something like, "I would be a great graduate student because . . ." with the rest of the paragraph backing up that topic sentence with specific accomplishments. For example, you may have a topic sentence like this: "I have maintained a strong GPA while balancing the demands of a twenty-hour-a-week job, volunteer work, and being actively involved in a research lab." Complete the paragraph with the details. Graduate school is extremely demanding, and students who have demonstrated that they can perform at a consistently high level while balancing competing demands on their time are clearly ready for the demands of grad school.

Most PhD programs are mentorship programs. You will take courses, but you will get much of your training by working with an individual faculty member. If your interests and/or experience overlap faculty members, you want to use a paragraph in your personal statement to indicate that and to indicate that you have done your homework. Make it clear that you have taken the time to read the research of that faculty member. Selecting programs with which you have a strong fit with the interests of one or more faculty members will enhance your applications because there are often far more qualified applicants than there are positions in next year's class. In such a situation, you will be far more competitive if your interests overlap the program's goals and the specific interests of a faculty member. Not only will you be more competitive if you are a good fit with a faculty member, but you are also likely to be more interested and committed to your education.

You can improve the chances that your application will be looked at seriously by identifying faculty that you may wish to study under and contacting them several months before you submit your application. A simple email will do, and it should be brief. Introduce yourself and express your interest in the faculty member's research. Let the faculty member know of your plan to apply for grad school and ask if the faculty member will be accepting new students into his/her lab. If the person is not accepting students, that may be a program that you cross off your list of applications. Applications cost money and take time, so it is best to focus on those programs that best fit your interests. The application fees are not outrageous (usually under $100), and universities will often waive them for students in need, but they do add up if you apply to many schools.

Contacting potential mentors months before you apply to graduate school tells the faculty members you know about the mentorship model of graduate school and have done your homework in identifying them as ideal mentors. In your personal statement, you can mention your earlier email and that you understand this faculty member is planning on accepting a student this year. This addition to the statement lets every faculty member who reads your statement know you are sophisticated, and it reminds the target faculty member of your earlier email. If you handle this well, at the very least you will impress the faculty members you contact, even if it does not result in an offer of admission.

Finally, avoid statements that cannot be backed up. Saying you are passionate about the subject matter will carry little weight unless you can point to a pattern of accomplishment and hard work to back up your passion. Saying that you are a leader means little if you have no history of leadership. In the same vein, avoid claiming accomplishments that have not yet happened. For example, many students are in the middle of planning a research study for their thesis during the application period. Far too many of them describe the timetable for an extensive study that could not possibly be accomplished in the time available, and the faculty reading such statements know how long a study takes. If your optimism is unrealistic, it will be a strike against you.

Your Letters of Recommendation

The letters of recommendation are critical in backing up your contention that you are a strong student capable of graduate work. At least one of those letters should be from a faculty member who has worked closely with you. In most cases, this will be a faculty member with whom you worked in their lab and perhaps who sponsored your senior or honors thesis. That person can speak about characteristics critical to success in graduate school but not necessarily visible in undergraduate classes. You should have at least one more letter from someone who knows you well enough to be able to speak about your strengths. It is fine to have a third letter from someone whose only contact with you was through a single course if you have other letters from people who know you well.

Ask your letter writers well in advance whether they would be willing to write you a letter. Most PhD applications are due around December 1, and the end of the first semester is a busy time for faculty. So do not spring your request a week before the letter is due.

Make it easy for your letter writers by providing background information about yourself, such as your résumé, perhaps a copy of the great paper you wrote in their class, and a list of everything they should know about you but may not remember when sitting down to write the letter. It is also helpful if you provide background information about the programs you wish to attend. Do not forget that more than just academics count in such letters. If you were a great student while also working two jobs, let your letter writers know. If you were promoted to management within six months after taking your part-time job, let them know. Most faculty want to be able to write strong letters for their students, and the more information they have available to back up that strong letter, the better.

Master's Programs

Not everyone interested in graduate training will want to earn a PhD. For some areas of study, a master's degree will give you the credentials you need to be successful in the field. In fact, in some areas, master's degrees are considered the norm, with few students earning a doctoral degree. You should be aware that in master's programs, unlike many PhD programs, stipend support is rare. Consequently, you will be getting your degree more quickly but likely spending more money in the process.

Because there is so much variability in master's programs, it is wise to do a lot of research on individual programs before you apply. Most programs have detailed websites, but programs are increasingly offering informational sessions. These sessions are often online, but live, so you can ask questions and listen to how faculty representatives respond to the questions of potential students. Do not be afraid to meet with a faculty representative or director of a master's program that looks interesting to you. These people are committed to getting the strongest students possible, so they are often willing to take the time to inform and possibly recruit a great student.

Master's degree programs differ dramatically from one field to another and from one university to another. Consequently, it is hard to state firm rules about the best way to approach your application for a master's program. I encourage you to talk with resource people at your university about the value of a master's degree and how it relates to your career goals.

There are two types of master's programs. One is an intentional terminal program, which means that the expectation is that the training will prepare you for your career without the necessity of additional training. These programs tend to be applied programs in which there are careers available for master's-level graduates. In fact, many of them are careers in which the master's degree is considered to be the appropriate terminal degree. We find such degrees for programs like business and school psychology. We will be covering the Masters of Business Administration (MBA) later in this chapter.

The second type of master's program is designed to provide basic graduate-level training that could prepare you for a career, add additional skills to help you be more successful in your current career, or demonstrate your potential for more advanced training in a PhD program. The websites for master's programs will usually make it clear the nature of their program. This information should guide your choices of programs. It is bad form to tell a program that expects to train people ready for a career that you want to do additional training after you complete their program. (Note that if you want to earn a PhD, the optimal strategy is to apply to PhD programs. You would normally earn your master's degree along the way. If you are doing reasonably well but not to the level expected of a PhD graduate, the program may insist that you leave after getting your master's degree [called a *terminal master's*].)

Master's programs are less likely to have the mentorship model found in most PhD programs. You may well do independent research as part of the requirements, but most of the work will be either classroom based or in the field. Some master's programs are small, much like PhD programs, but others often take large incoming classes and run several sections of each required course. Many MBA programs are of this nature. They provide a higher level of training in business subjects in classes that include a more select group of students.

Being More Competitive

Because the models of education vary more in master's programs than PhD programs, there are fewer clear rules on how to be more competitive for admission. Good scores (grades and admissions tests) help but are rarely the deciding factor. Letters can carry a lot of weight, especially if your scores are lower than those of the average student granted admission. Because master's programs tend to be less competitive than PhD programs, the minimum scores tend to be lower and the number of applicants for each available position also tends to be lower.

Master's programs that are designed to train you for an applied career often like to see evidence that you have the social skills needed for that career. You can demonstrate such skills with work or volunteer experience in socially demanding situations, especially if your performance on that work is backed up with one of your letters of recommendation.

Finally, some master's programs are designed to be part time. This is true of many education programs in which teachers take one to three advanced courses a year. Admission to these programs is relatively easy if you have a solid undergraduate degree and are employed in the field. The nature of these programs is that they strengthen the qualifications of their students to do their job better. There is also less of an expectation that every student will complete all the requirements of a master's degree. Students take courses when they are beneficial to the student's career objectives and when their time, energy, and money permit them to take the courses.

Law School, Medical School, and MBA Programs

Most law schools, medical schools, and MBA programs take larger classes than the typical PhD program. These programs range from competitive to extremely competitive for admission. The more competitive the program, generally the more prestigious the degree is when you complete the program.

Most of these programs do not follow a mentorship model, so the application package is more standardized.

Medical School

The deadlines for application to medical school vary by school, but they tend to be ten to twelve months before medical school classes begin. Most, but not all, medical schools in the United States use the American Medical College Application Service (AMCAS) to gather the information for student applications and then forward it to the schools to which the student wants to apply. The application package will include the Medical College Application Test (MCAT), your college transcript detailing that you have completed all the premed courses, and a personal statement. Most schools also require a background check because licensing laws in most states will exclude any medical school graduate with a criminal background. Finally, many programs require interviews of their top candidates before making firm offers of admission.

Most medical schools offer the MD (Doctor of Medicine) degree, but some programs also offer combination degrees. The MD/PhD programs train people to be both physicians and medical researchers. The MD/MBA programs train people to be both physicians and businesspeople (usually medical administrators). If this is the direction you want to go, I encourage you to contact these programs directly and do it early in your undergraduate career to learn what they want from their applicants.

Medical schools vary dramatically on how they handle admissions, so it would be a good idea to start exploring potential schools as early as your sophomore year and take notes on application deadlines and options. Many schools offer early admission to strong students, which is great for both the student and the school. For the student, early admission eases the stress of the admissions process. For the schools, early admission guarantees that part of their class is already filled with strong applicants. Note that if you have accepted early admission to a program, you have made a commitment, and deciding to apply to other schools is not acceptable.

An alternative to the MD degree is the DO degree (Doctor of Osteopathic Medicine). There are fewer programs that offer the DO degree than the MD degree, and those programs are a bit less competitive. Training is similar, and licensing laws apply equally in all fifty states. The DO degree tends to have more training in alternative medicine, although most of the training is in traditional medicine, and people with DO degrees tend to go into primary care rather than a specialty.

The field of medicine is huge and has been changing rapidly for decades. In addition to the doctors, there are professionals at many different levels. If the field of medicine intrigues you but the idea of spending seven or more years in training (med school plus a residency) does not, there are many other options that are worth exploring. You may want to investigate programs such as physician's assistants (PA), nursing, nurse practitioners (NP), or physical therapy (PT).

Law School

The degree awarded after completing law school is the JD degree (Juris Doctor). Law school applications are handled differently than graduate school applications. Unlike PhD programs, which review all the applications at one time, law school applications are typically handled on a rolling admission basis. The application portal typically opens around the beginning of the fall semester and closes near the end of the fall semester for a class that starts the next fall. Like medical schools, law schools range from competitive to extremely competitive, and the more competitive the program, the more prestigious the degree.

Virtually every law school requires the LSAT (Law School Admissions Test) as part of the application process. Unlike the GRE, there is no math section on the LSAT, but there is a writing section. The other section includes multiple-choice questions to evaluate elements like reading comprehension and reasoning skills.

There are recommended college courses to prepare you for law school. These pre-law courses are a bit less formal than the premed course programs, but students are well advised to follow those recommendations. Because there is more flexibility in the prelaw program compared to the premed program, you will find law school applicants with a wider range of undergraduate majors. Many students use their major to prepare them for specialization in their intended legal careers. For example, those individuals who would like to practice family law may choose to major or minor in fields such as psychology or education. Those who plan to practice criminal law are more likely to major or minor in criminal justice. Those planning on practicing corporate law are more interested in business background. This is a case in which the undergraduate majors and minors can add a significant level of expertise that will improve the competitive edge for law school graduates.

Michael Raulin

The range of careers for law school graduates is wider than the range for medical school graduates. Most medical school graduates will go into the practice of medicine, but a significant subset of law school graduates goes into other fields in which their legal sophistication will give them a competitive edge. For example, specialists in finance and the markets can be more effective in handling mergers if they also have basic legal training. They may still hire attorneys to handle the legal aspects of a merger, but with their background, they can communicate more effectively with the attorneys and integrate the goals of the merger better with the legal requirements of such a corporate move.

MBA Programs

MBA programs have been an entry-level credential to high-level corporate careers for decades. Once rather rare, the number of MBA degrees has been increasing, especially with the advent of online MBA programs. Most MBA programs will take two years to complete if you attend full time. Some of those traditional programs also offer a night program that typically takes four years. This option is ideal for someone who works full time but wants to get credentials that will open avenues for advancement. Recently, there has been an explosion of online MBA programs. Because most of these programs are so new, they often do not have the track record that allows you to evaluate how the programs are judged by potential employers.

Although there are no hard-and-fast rules about the value of an MBA, a general principle is the more competitive the admissions process for a program, the more prestigious the degree when you finish. Also be aware that an MBA is more valuable if it is combined with real-world experience. The very best programs are typically housed at top private universities, although there are a few prestigious public universities on that list. A degree from one of those programs will all but guarantee visits from top corporations searching for the best possible talent.

The MBA is a lucrative degree for universities. The tuition is typically high, but the cost of specialized facilities, such as labs, is much lower than it is for other graduate programs. Moreover, the

132

expected income of graduates is high enough that such high tuition does not scare students away. What this means is that there is enormous variability in the quality of MBA programs and the competitiveness of those programs for admissions. A strong and competitive program will be an invaluable asset; a weaker program that takes almost anyone who applies may not be worth the price of tuition. This situation is perhaps expressed best by a famous Groucho Marx quotation: "I do not want to belong to a club that would accept me as a member."

If you want a career in business, especially if you want to work for large corporations, an MBA from a strong program will often put you on the fast track for success. It is less clear if an MBA will carry much weight in smaller companies, which typically cannot afford the high salaries paid to MBA graduates paid by larger corporations.

Deadlines for MBA applications vary widely and are roughly correlated with the degree of selectivity of the program. The more selective the program, the more likely that the deadlines are earlier. That may partly reflect that the most selective programs receive many applications and can only accept a small portion of the applicants. Most MBA programs require the GMAT (Graduate Management Admissions Test), although some programs will also accept the GRE (Graduate Record Exam), which is typically used for PhD applications. Some schools will waive the GMAT if you have substantial data to support your readiness for the program. Unlike PhD programs, which rely heavily on letters of recommendation, many MBA programs make those letters optional or do not accept them at all.

Most MBA students have undergraduate training in business and/or experience working in business settings. Although schools do not restrict admissions to business undergraduates, it can be challenging in your first year to take an accounting course when more than 90 percent of the students in the class are taking their third accounting course and this is your first accounting course.

Although most MBA programs focus on preparing students for business careers, several programs have alternative tracks. For example, running a nonprofit organization requires the same business skills as running a business. The focus may not be on maximizing profit, but business skills will help with the management of hiring, investment, expansion, and grant writing. There are also programs that specialize in medical management for hospitals and large medical practices. The principles of business are the same as with any other company, but the unique demands of medical settings require specialized skills and knowledge.

MBA programs vary widely on many dimensions, and there are many options available. Application deadlines and application packages also vary from one school to another. Therefore, it is wise to do your homework and do it early (such as during your sophomore year). The information will allow you to focus on those factors most relevant for the programs you want to attend and to plan your schedule for submitting applications and the supporting material.

Being More Competitive

Law school, medical school, and MBA programs are clearly different from one another, but they share one thing in common that separates them from most graduate schools: they accept large classes. This means they tend to rely more on scores (GPA and admissions tests) and personal statements and experience. Sometimes, the personal experiences are listed in a résumé, which is a common requirement in MBA programs. Often, such experiences are emphasized in the personal statement.

It is common for schools offering MD, JD, and MBA degrees to have rolling admissions. In most cases, getting your application in early is an advantage. However, virtually every school insists that they will not even consider your application unless it is complete. Therefore, you will want to list each school of interest, what each school wants, and when they want it for the application. Your senior year is going to be busy, so you want to have everything ready to go for your applications before that year starts.

Chapter Summary

Many careers require graduate or professional education, and most of those programs are competitive. Moreover, the deadlines for many of those programs are six to ten months before the start of classes, so you need to be thinking about these applications early in your junior year of college to be ready to submit them in time. Each program is different in terms of what they are looking for in applicants. You will want to begin exploring these programs in your sophomore year to learn what they expect from applicants and to begin building the academic record that will make you competitive.

The more competitive the admissions process for a school, the more prestigious and valuable your degree will be. The relationship between the prestige of the program and the deadline date for applications may not be as strong, but you should expect earlier deadlines for the most competitive programs. Again, if you want to be competitive, you should start thinking about where you want to go early and take steps to have the strongest application package possible by the application deadline.

Chapter 11
Planning for a Career

P lanning for a career used to be easier. There were far fewer careers to choose from, and most careers lasted for more than a decade or two. Life is more complicated now, at least in terms of planning for careers.

There are still great careers out there, and there are new options being created all the time. When I started as a college professor, I often taught courses in introductory psychology. In those courses, I routinely talked about how the average person would have three separate careers over the course of their working life. That was true, but mostly because blue-collar workers were forced to change careers frequently. At the time, most professionals and white-collar workers tended to stay in the same career or have two careers over the course of their lifetime. Now, change is almost inevitable for everyone regardless of their occupation. Moreover, even if you stay in the same occupation, what you will be doing will be so dramatically different by the time you reach retirement age that for all practical purposes, you will have entered a new career.

The volatility and rapid change in the job market mean that planning for a career is difficult and that a good plan needs to be flexible. If I had a crystal ball, one that actually worked, I would be happy to share with you what will happen over the next fifty years. I do not have such a device, and those people brave enough to make long-term predictions have consistently done poorly in those predictions. Consequently, this chapter will not tell you what to do, but rather will lay out strategies to help you prepare yourself for your first career and for whatever transitions you will be required to make, or you choose to make, during your working life.

Your First Career

Some careers are directly tied to your major in college. If you are majoring in business or engineering or education, I assume that you selected your major because that is the field you want to go into. Other majors are less directly tied to your first job, but they may be tied to a range of careers. Still other majors are tied to preparing you for advanced training in graduate or professional schools. Regardless of whether your current major is tied narrowly to a specific career, it is to your advantage to be thinking in terms of careers. The point of college is to give you a competitive edge for whatever job or advanced training option is right for you. Finishing as one of the top people in your class is certainly a competitive edge, but there are other ways of obtaining a competitive edge.

One way to plan your college courses is to imagine yourself in your first job interview. Your potential employer is almost certainly interviewing several people for the same position. What can you say in response to their questions that tell the interviewers that you are both better prepared and the most viable candidate? Clearly, you want an impressive academic record, but what else would make you stand out? Which minors would give you the edge in that job interview? Some minors would clearly give you skills that would be valuable in your first job and position you for rapid advancement; other minors may not be as impressive to those interviewing you for a job.

We talked about how specific courses and/or work experiences will give you skills that are almost uniformly valuable. These include courses in technology and computers, basic business courses, and courses that enhance communication skills. Beyond courses, volunteer or work experiences that demonstrate leadership potential, responsibility, organizational skills, and the ability to work with people all strengthen your application. We have stressed these elements because students often overlook them in applying for advanced training or their first job. A good academic record is valuable; couple it with these other factors, and you will have a great application package.

Michael Raulin

There is a well-validated psychological principle that the best predictor of future behavior is past behavior in a similar situation. Keep that principle in mind throughout your college career as you decide how to use your time. Do not just think in terms of courses; rather, think in terms of experiences. Doing well in courses is valuable because it suggests that you have high standards and are willing to work hard to achieve those standards. However, those courses likely have little in common with what the work world expects on a day-to-day basis. You can significantly enhance your application by being able to tell the interviewer about your successes in areas that are more closely related to the job.

Future Careers

No matter what career you are training for in school, it is a good bet that you will work in other fields before retirement. It is also a good bet that you may well be working in a field that does not even exist now. Almost half of the fields that currently employ people today did not exist when I was in college, and the fields that did exist then are so different from what they were back then that for all practical purposes, they represent new careers. How can one possibly plan for future careers when you have no idea what those careers may be?

The simple answer to the above question is that it is impossible to plan for something you cannot predict. Later in this chapter, we will talk about skills that will never go out of fashion; these skills will be beneficial no matter what field you select. Two other traits that will prepare you for future careers are an open mind and a willingness to continue to learn.

Individuals with an open mind are willing to consider new opportunities. They are willing to imagine that they can take on new challenges, be successful, and enjoy those new challenges. Moreover, when an opportunity occurs, they often take the opportunity. That does not mean that everything they try works out or that they enjoy everything that they try. But a willingness to try is so important in a world that is unpredictable and constantly changing.

138

Earlier I said that the most valuable skill one learns in college is to think clearly, and I stand by that statement. The willingness to learn and the confidence that one can learn is both an attitude and a skill. Almost everything you learn in college will be outdated before you reach retirement, and some of it will be outdated much sooner than that. If you do not continue to learn, you will fail in whatever career you choose. Some of you may consider that far too strong a statement, but the data supports this contention. You may do fine when the economy is strong and there is enough work for everyone. The problem occurs when the economy takes a downturn, which it always does periodically. That is when those who have not kept up with the field will be the first to be let go.

Do not think you can avoid this pressure by being an independent professional. Their clients disappear quickly when the best people in the field suddenly have the time to take on new clients. You may find it scary to realize that failing to keep up with a field can doom your chances of long-term success. However, you can look at this principle from another angle. The best people in the field, the people who are always on the cutting edge, easily weather periodic downturns. Staying current is the best career insurance you can buy.

Virtually everything I learned in college and graduate school is outdated, but I am proud to say that I have stayed on the cutting-edge throughout my career. Quite frankly, things were moving more slowly thirty years ago than they are moving for you right now. Technology is leading to monumental changes in how we do things and how we think about things, and that technology is having a huge impact on every career. As I write this, self-driving cars and trucks are already a reality and could become commonplace soon. There are trucks on the road right now being driven by computers with a backup truck driver sitting behind the wheel but doing nothing but watching. The number of jobs for truck drivers will decrease dramatically once a machine can reliably drive as safely as a human driver and not need to stop for bathroom breaks or to eat and sleep.

The same is true for the most sophisticated of careers. Even the best-trained professionals are unable to achieve the level of reliability and accuracy that is already available through artificial intelligence (Kahneman, Sibony, & Sunstein, 2021). It may not be long before radiologists are no longer the people who read the X-rays and MRIs in the hospital. It may not be long before machine intelligence becomes the underwriters for insurance policies, accurately setting fees that balance risk against competition from other companies. It may not be long before hiring decisions are made based on standardized machine assessment rather than human interviews. We are seeing dramatic changes in every aspect of our life today because of advances in artificial intelligence. Even football has been changing. The principles that once guided coaches on what plays to call have been upended by the statistics that are available to coaches today. Even ten years ago, it was rare for a coach to consider going for it on fourth down. However, such decisions have become routine based on the statistical analysis of costs and benefits.

It is easy to feel overwhelmed when you imagine that your task in college is preparing for something that you cannot predict. It is a brave new world in front of us, and that world has enormous potential for those individuals courageous enough and open-minded enough to take on the new challenges. It may be that the decision of when to retire will rely less on one's health and more on one's willingness to continue to learn and adapt to inevitable change.

Preparing to be Flexible

The traditional model of a broad college education was based on the idea that such broad training would prepare you to think clearly and work in many different areas. Many students elect programs that differ from this traditional model because those programs train them for specific careers that require extensive specialization. The traditionalists sometimes argue that such programs are sellouts, but I disagree. The world is exceedingly complex, and the careers on which our world is built require specialization, and sometimes extensive specialization. I have no trouble with engineers knowing a lot about engineering. Frankly, I do not want my bridges built by people who do not know a lot about engineering. The compromise in such programs is that students may not receive the broader education that gives them an expanded perspective and prepares them for shifts in their careers and in their lives.

I encourage all students, however, to expect that their occupations will change and that it is possible that their occupations will change many times. The goal in college is to prepare yourself to move quickly to pursue new directions that are in your best interest. For most careers, promotions mean taking leadership roles. It is rare that you will find a course in the college catalog entitled Leadership. But there are ways of developing leadership skills or developing the skills that will be needed in a leadership position through your selection of courses or activities.

Leadership involves understanding and motivating people, and selected psychology courses can help with those skills. Leadership involves systematically analyzing options, reviewing data regarding those options, and making the best possible decisions. Courses in logic, critical thinking, and statistical analysis may well strengthen those skills. Frankly, some of the skills you may need twenty-five years from now do not exist yet, so they are certainly not a part of a standard college course catalog. But the more skills you have, the more flexible you will be in your career. Moreover, the more you know, the easier it is to learn new things. When it comes to constantly educating yourself, the rich (i.e., those already well educated) truly do get richer.

Skills that Never Go Out of Fashion

My apologies for being repetitious in this section, but sometimes repetition is good. The most important skill you can get in college is to learn to think clearly and critically. That skill will never go out of style. You will find courses specifically designed to do that; in most universities, they are typically taught in the philosophy department. However, thinking critically can and should be learned in every college course that you take. Do not just try to absorb the information in your courses; try to process it, challenge it, and understand where it came from. Those habits will serve you well throughout college and throughout your life.

We devoted an entire chapter to communication skills. If you have two people who are equally skilled at critical analysis and one is a better communicator, that one will almost certainly be the more successful individual. Great ideas do not count unless they can be communicated in a manner that convinces people of their greatness. Most successful people write clearly and speak persuasively, and generally they developed those skills because they focused on developing them. Like so many things in life, communication skills require practice.

Leadership skills are always valuable, even if your current position is not one of leadership. Leadership is not the skill of giving orders. Leadership involves understanding people and their motives and being able to encourage people to work toward common goals. I have never met a good leader who was simply bossy; I have, however, met leaders who were direct but were able to instill confidence in people to follow their direction.

There may not be courses on how to be a good leader, but increasingly, universities are offering certificates in leadership or leadership endorsements. Moreover, there are always opportunities in courses to take a leadership position. For example, many students like to study together, and within that strategy, there are many opportunities to practice the skills of a leader. What are the goals of the group? Does everyone in the group have the same goals? What are the best ways to achieve those goals? How do we overcome the inevitable challenges? Those are the questions a good leader instinctively asks. In a study group, it would be bad form to tell people what they must do. However, it would be great form to raise those questions openly. When you do, everyone in the group will see that you have the vision to be the group leader.

Chapter Summary

You will likely devote considerable energy in college to preparing for a specific career. Advisors will help you prepare, but you can take more control over your college education by imagining being interviewed for your ideal position at the end of college. What can you do now that will give you strong arguments to the question of why you would be the best person for the job? The answer may be the courses you took in addition to the courses for your major and your minor. However, your work and volunteer experiences may be even more important. They may not only teach you valuable skills but also provide strong evidence that you possess those skills.

In today's rapidly changing world, you can expect to have more than one career or for your chosen career to change dramatically over time. To be successful, you need to be open-minded, willing to learn, and flexible. You may not be able to predict the various directions your career may take, but you can prepare yourself to adapt to the inevitable changes in the career landscape. Some skills will be useful no matter what direction your career takes. These include clear thinking, excellent communication skills, and solid leadership experience.

Section III
Mentors and Beyond

O ne of the most powerful themes in the biographies of successful people is that they had excellent mentors. Mentors are an invaluable resource. They guide us to make wise decisions and to avoid disastrous decisions. They inspire us to believe in ourselves while also encouraging us to improve and grow. They are a source of emotional support and an emotional anchor during turbulent times.

Most of the best mentors were themselves mentored. In fact, there are few mentors who have not been mentored. But the process of mentorship is unlike every other form of self-improvement. If you want to improve your writing skills, you may sign up for courses in writing or hire a tutor or copyeditor to improve your writing. Because writing is so important to professional success, most universities have writing programs available to any student who wants to use them. But mentors do not list their services and course schedules or hang out a shingle offering to provide those services for a fee. Instead, most mentor/mentee relationships develop in the context of work or school.

To be successful, a mentorship relationship should be symbiotic. In fact, I would argue that all good relationships are symbiotic. The basis of the symbiosis for a mentorship relationship is that mentors want to improve your performance because it helps them in their work. This is especially true if you are working with your mentor on research. But there is a second reason mentors benefit from doing their job well. If they are successful at mentoring people, they will be able to attract other outstanding people to work with them. Finally, the professional who successfully mentors other professionals is widely recognized, not just for their professional achievements, but also for their

144

contributions in helping to shape some of the most productive people in the company or field.

There is no question that a good mentor is enormously valuable. Although it is possible that you can be successful without good mentorship, the likelihood is lower than it would be with a mentor. Therefore, finding good mentors is worth the effort. In the chapters that follow, we will help you understand the basis of successful mentorship relationships, how to be more competitive for the best mentors, and how to reward the mentors for their time in helping you to be more successful.

Successful professionals typically have several mentors at various points in their training and career. In chapter 12, we start by talking about mentors in college. These are often faculty members, but they do not have to be. Graduate students at universities can be excellent mentors for undergraduate students, and even advanced students can be excellent mentors for younger students. A faculty advisor is a mentor, but often the advisor only meets with his or her students a couple of times a year. Any college instructor could be a mentor, but most do not see their primary job as mentoring students. Instead, they see their job as teaching. Both advisors and instructors are helpful, but not nearly as helpful as working closely with a faculty mentor on major projects.

As important as college mentors are, the mentors you select after graduating will likely be far more important to your career success. They are often very successful themselves, but they are great mentors only if they are committed to the success of others. Chapter 12 also talks about such career mentors, how to find them, and how to convince them that you are worthy of their time, energy, and wisdom.

Most people believe that the word *commencement* means "finishing" because we use that term to refer to the ceremony after graduating from high school or college. But the word actually means "beginning." College is not the goal; it is the method that prepares you for real life. Education does not even require school; all it requires is access to information and people who can help you master that information. If you want to be successful, you must commit to life-long learning. Career mentors emphasize such learning, but they also shape other critical skills and attitudes. For example, they teach you to deal with strategies, planning, adapting, and working with others.

You may find chapter 13 surprising because it focuses on how to become a mentor. This may seem to be far beyond the scope of this book. It may even deserve a book of its own, but it fits in perfectly with the goals of this book. You learned earlier that the best way to learn things is to focus on learning the material so you can teach it to others. This is a powerful effect. In a similar way, the best way to truly benefit from being mentored is to imagine yourself in the mentor role, or better yet, actually be a mentor. You will develop faster in a mentorship relationship if you are actively processing the interactions to better understand how you can be a more effective mentor.

The last two chapters of this book deal with issues often overlooked in college and career advice books. There are some career directions that only require intense focus for a few years. For example, many athletic careers require skills that deteriorate quickly with age. But most careers last longer and are successful only if you can maintain focus and effectiveness for decades. Achieving success requires hard work, dedication, and emotional strength. The success itself is often motivating enough to help people to maintain that level of dedication, but few people can be successful over decades without a strong support structure and a balance in their lives.

A few successful people may have been able to succeed on drive alone, but very few. It is common for professionals to work ungodly hours in graduate or professional school and in the early years of their career. It is difficult to maintain a family life and other sources of support and balance during those years. But the truly successful professionals find a way to keep their sense of equilibrium through close relationships, meaningful activities, and a sense of purpose. Unfortunately, there are no college courses on how to do that, although there are several courses that provide ideas on how some people have found such balance in the past.

146

You will find this last section less proscriptive than earlier sections of the book. That is because there are fewer strategies that work for everyone. The focus of these last few chapters is to outline your goals and some possible ways to facilitate your effort to achieve those goals. But personal goals are a rich mosaic, which differ dramatically from one person to another. My goal in this last section is to help you to identify what you are looking for. I am confident that if you create your own pathway in life, you will be able to find the elements that help you stay on that path when necessary and alter your direction when necessary, all while riding out the inevitable bumps in the roads.

Chapter 12
Finding Mentors

A mentor is someone who provides advice, feedback, and guidance on how to best achieve your goals. In college, the people most likely to be your mentors are your advisors, your instructors, and academic employers. However, you need not limit yourself to just these individuals. A knowledgeable student may make an excellent mentor, and many of the administrative assistants who make departments run smoothly can often be excellent mentors. Note also that you need not be in physical contact with someone for them to be a mentor. Online communities often provide excellent opportunities for shared experiences and mentorship. Books such as this one can provide a mentorship role without you ever meeting the author, and information from discussion boards may prove invaluable in helping you to make decisions about your future. Most universities have professional advisors, who can be particularly valuable early in your college career as mentors.

Mentorship continues well beyond college. In fact, the most important mentors for professionals are the people who shape their development during their early career development. The nature of the mentorship role changes after college, but the importance of mentorship never decreases. It is rare that people who are successful in their professional careers have not had several mentors during that career.

In this chapter, we will focus on the value of mentors, the most common places to find and cultivate a mentorship relationship, and ways to use mentorship to increase the effectiveness of your decisions.

The Nature of Mentor Relationships

There is no single model for mentorship. There also is no precise definition of what constitutes a mentor. The mentors in our life may range from people providing helpful advice to people helping us at almost every stage of our development. They also range from being deliberate mentors, who carefully guide us, to individuals who model effective strategies, often without being aware that they are providing guidance.

Mentors in College

Mentors come in all shapes and sizes, and they influence us in different ways at different times in our lives. In this section, I will review the most common source of mentorship in college and how best to use that information.

Family Members

Our first mentors are often our parents or other family members. Some parents are amazing mentors, while other parents provide little or no mentorship. Some parents may even provide their mentorship by being excellent counterexamples (i.e., role models of what not to do). *Parents* here are defined as the people who parent us; these are not always our biological parents. I include in this group older siblings, grandparents, and any other family members who provide emotional support and guidance. If your parents have been good mentors, you should be thankful. However, even the best of parents can only provide so much mentorship to their children. We all need to learn from many different people as we develop into the adults we want to be.

If you are reading this book as you are about to head off to college or just starting college, the value of your parental mentorship may be at a low point. In normal development, teenagers need to break away and establish their independence from their parents. This breaking away can be frustrating and uncomfortable, but if there has been a basic loving relationship between parents and their children, the relationship will survive and in time flourish again.

One of my favorite quotations, which is attributed to Mark Twain, goes like this: "When I was seventeen, my father was so stupid I was embarrassed to be seen with him. But by the time I was twenty-two, I was amazed at how much he had learned in just five short years." Mark Twain had a way of capturing truth with a sense of humor. So right now, your parents may not be your primary mentor; they may never be a primary mentor again. But hopefully, they provided mentorship when you needed it early in life and will continue to provide emotional support and love as you proceed through life.

Advisors

Your first mentor in college is likely to be the person assigned to you as your advisor. Universities handle advisement responsibilities in different ways. Some universities have full-time advisors who are thoroughly knowledgeable in certain areas of study and devote their entire time and energy to helping students make academic decisions and excel in college. Other universities will assign students to a faculty member in the student's major department. Finally, some universities provide advisement services when students ask. These universities typically create advisement departments that the students can visit whenever they have a question.

The academic advisor in college serves many roles, depending upon the stage of the student's career. In the first year or two, your advisor will typically give you information about required courses and advice on courses that may serve your personal long-term goals. As you progress, you will not need such basic advice, and the role of the advisor will change. The advisor may spend more time helping you with career planning than with course selection. Advisors may be able and willing to help with more personal issues, but you should not count on that. For example, if you are experiencing emotional problems or problems with drugs and alcohol, academic advisors are more likely to refer you to experts than to try to be of help themselves.

Again, depending on the university, you may need your advisor to sign off on some of your decisions. For example, many universities require, for at least two years, that your course selection be approved by an advisor. If you are doing well, that requirement is dropped at some point. However, if you are having trouble with your schoolwork, the university will typically require that your advisor continue to help you make good decisions about your academic career. The advisor may also be helpful in providing information on how to get into courses that require special permission. In some cases, the advisor may be able to give the required permission, but in most cases, the permission will be granted by someone else in the university.

Advisors vary dramatically on how much they can or are willing to do for student. Some strictly give information and provide the necessary signatures to authorize the student to take courses. Some are also willing to give advice and support. Some are willing to be a resource person to the student. How well the advisor functions with you will be partly dependent on how well the two of you connect. If you work at building a good relationship with your advisors, you are more likely to find them helpful when you need the help.

There may be times when the interpersonal fit between a student and advisor is so bad that the relationship is not working. If that happens for you, check to see if a change in advisors is possible. There is no rule that says that the only person who can give you advice in college is your advisor! In fact, the rest of this section will talk about the other people who may be valuable mentors and advisors.

Faculty

Every course you take in college will have an instructor. The instructor may be a tenured faculty member with an international reputation, or a graduate student employed to teach the course. The instructor may work full time for the university teaching and doing research or may be employed by the university to teach that course only. You already know that some teachers are better at their jobs than others. You also know that some teachers are more inspiring than others. Finally, you know that some faculty are more accessible and open to talking with students than others.

Virtually every instructor is willing to answer questions about the course and related materials. If you find an instructor interesting or even inspiring, I encourage you to approach the instructor. If that thought intimidates you, there are ways of doing it that work well. For example, you may approach the instructor first by saying that you are enjoying and are excited by the course. How could any instructor not respond well to that? Then simply ask if the instructor will point you in the right direction to explore the topics of the course in more depth. That may include additional reading or access to resources available online. It may include suggestions on additional courses that would be helpful or other resource people who could be helpful. It may even lead to an invitation to work more closely with the faculty member in their lab. At the very least, you will have made a connection that goes beyond the typical instructor/student relationship.

Occasionally, you will have instructors that do not inspire you in the classroom. Consequently, you are reluctant to seek their advice outside of class. It can sometimes be helpful to meet with them during their office hours to ask questions about things you do not understand. You may be surprised at how different instructors can be in their office compared to the classroom.

In chapter 9, we talked about the importance of an intensive learning experience with a faculty member in your field. Typically, that involves working in their lab or working with them on scholarly projects. This is the single best mentorship opportunity that most students experience in their undergraduate career. Not only are you getting a taste for what graduate and professional schools are going to be like, but also you are learning things that could never be learned in a traditional classroom. Moreover, you are getting to know a faculty member at a level rarely experienced by undergraduate students. This is much closer to the experience of being a graduate student.

I cannot speak for all faculty members, but my experience is that most faculty members who include undergraduate students in their labs or their other scholarly work view themselves as mentors and put tremendous energy into serving in that role. They not only will help you build skills that will prepare you for professional or graduate school, but they are also likely to give you information about how to be more competitive in your applications. Finally, they will do their best through a letter of recommendation to give you the best chance to get into advanced training programs. Now, in full disclosure, all of that depends on how well you perform in working with the faculty member. Letters of recommendation cover more than just talent; they include comments on your attitude, dependability, and attention to detail. If your work is mediocre, the faculty member would be hard-pressed to write you a strong letter of recommendation and would be less likely to want to invest time into your professional development.

Campus Employers

It is common for students to be employed on campus. Sometimes the employment is part of a student aid package, but often the employment is a symbiotic relationship between the university and the student. The student is on campus, so campus employment is convenient, and typically the best students on campus are the ones most likely to get these jobs. Some of the jobs do not require constant attention and allow the students to study in between their duties. That is another advantage of these jobs. Yet a third advantage is that many universities give student employees priority in registering for classes. This can be handy if you are trying to get into a course that typically fills quickly.

Students rarely see these jobs as an opportunity for mentorship, but they can be. For example, many of the jobs on campus will put you in contact with faculty members on a regular basis. If you do your job well and maintain a good relationship with one or more faculty members, they can be very helpful when you have questions or want to run an idea by them. Even when your job does not have direct contact with faculty members, you are likely to be in contact with people who know the university and often have wonderful contacts within the university. They can provide great advice and the contacts to open opportunities that may not otherwise be available to you.

Students

Most students cannot imagine other students as being suitable mentors, but a mentor is defined as anyone who can provide the support and guidance that will help you reach your goals. It is entirely possible for a student to be a mentor, especially if the student is more senior than you. For example, seniors applying to graduate school will likely know what graduate schools are looking for, information that you may not know as a sophomore. They may have learned the hard way how to be more competitive for graduate school. I say the hard way because they learned too late to build the credentials that would have helped. But if they share that information, you may be able to learn from their mistake.

If you are attending college at a major university, you are likely to have contact with graduate students. In fact, some of those graduate students may be teaching some of your undergraduate courses. If you are working in a faculty member's lab, you are likely to have close contact with several graduate students. Graduate students were serious undergraduates who put together records that were strong enough to get them admitted to graduate school. Most are happy to answer your questions about their experiences in applying to graduate school.

This is a good time to make a point that will become obvious in the next chapter. The line between mentor and mentee is not absolute. Most people provide the kind of advice and support to others that make them a mentor while at the same time receiving advice and support from someone else. Earlier in this book, I noted that the best way to learn something is to learn it in a way that would allow you to teach it to someone else. The best way to utilize mentors is to learn how to be one yourself. That does not mean that you should go around giving advice to every student who is less senior than you. That approach is not likely to win friends or influence people. In fact, it may just irritate those people. But if you are open to the idea, you will be surprised how many people recognize that you are a leader and a potentially good mentor and seek you out. Not only does it feel good to be viewed as a potential mentor, but it is also great training for becoming the professional you want to be.

Staff

We mentioned earlier that your employer on campus may be a valuable source of advice and information. Almost anyone at the university could play that role. The staff that run department offices often have been at the university for years or even decades. They know the university well, and more importantly, they know who at the university can solve specific problems. In my own experience, the administrative assistant for the department is typically far more knowledgeable than the department chair when it comes to knowing how to get things done. For that reason, I make sure that I have a good relationship with them. That is not the only reason I have a good relationship with them. These are often talented, hard-working, and interesting people, well worth knowing for the conversation value alone.

I would not recommend that you get advice on which graduate programs would best serve your career goals from the administrative assistant in your department. Your faculty advisor or faculty mentor is far more likely to be able to answer that question. But if there was a course that I wanted to get into that never seems to be open when it is my time to register, I would start with the administrative assistant for the department to find a strategy for getting one of those coveted slots.

Mentors Beyond College

This section deserves far more then part of one chapter. There have been whole books written about mentorship in careers, and there is no way that I can adequately cover all that material here. But to fully understand the concept of mentorship, you need to realize that it will remain important throughout your career. As you become more sophisticated, as you move up the ladder, as you come closer to your ultimate career goals, the nature of the mentorship you receive will change, but the need for mentorship will not decrease.

Supervisor versus Mentor

Every supervisor is a potential mentor, but many supervisors are not up to that task. It takes confidence to be a mentor. The goal of the mentor is to help the people being mentored to be the best they can be. Supervisors who are concerned about being replaced are unlikely to want to groom the person who could easily be their replacement. Supervisors who feel confident are less concerned with you replacing them and instead think in terms of you taking over their position when they move up.

I know that it is not politically correct, but the world is competitive, and denying that or seeing competition as evil will handicap your career ambitions. However, one does not have to crawl over people to succeed. That is one of the misconceptions that turn this issue into one of political correctness. Excellent mentors are often on the fast track to success even as they dramatically improve the performance of those they mentor. People tend to think of success as an individual accomplishment, but it is better conceptualized as a team sport. Successful people not only perform well but manage at the same time to enhance the performance of the people around them.

Depth versus Breadth of Experience

The best organizations are constantly grooming people for high-level management positions. Grooming involves mentoring people in each of the phases of the company's operation so the individual can manage the entire operation when the time comes. The key to this kind of mentorship is that individuals must be willing and able to make repeated lateral shifts. These are not promotions but rather an opportunity for the person to learn another aspect of the company's operation. If you have already been selected for such grooming, the odds are good that the rationale for these constant moves from one department to the next has been explained to you.

But let's assume that you have not been identified as the person to be groomed for management, but you would like to position yourself for advancement. It would be to your advantage to seek out opportunities for these lateral moves and to work with the people in charge of these programs to provide the kind of mentorship that would prepare you for higher-level positions. Even if you were not selected early in your career as someone suitable for advancement, that does not mean that you cannot actively seek advancement by doing the same things the people who are being groomed for those positions are doing. There is nothing that says that you cannot seek out good mentors and reward them for their efforts in mentoring you with your performance and gratitude.

The two previous paragraphs focused on the role of mentorship in corporations, but mentorship can occur in any type of organization. In corporations, the typical promotion involves being responsible for increasingly large numbers of people and increasingly more of the operation of the company. That may be true in other organizations but not always. For example, in an academic environment, some faculty members would like to go on to be chair of the department or dean of the college or president of the university. However, for many faculty members, that is not their idea of success. Their idea of success is to be an effective scholar or teacher, recognized by their peers in the university and beyond. Senior faculty members who have achieved that goal can be outstanding mentors, helping a new faculty member set priorities and find procedures that are more effective in increasing productivity.

Again, the important point here is that mentors can be valuable throughout your entire professional life. Not every top individual in an organization wants to be a mentor, but many find the role flattering and rewarding and with just a little encouragement from you would be happy to provide the mentorship you are seeking.

Chapter Summary

The most valuable resource you can have in college and beyond is the availability of good mentors. It is normal for students and professionals to have several mentors over their career. People find mentors for the areas they want to develop at the time they want to develop those areas.

Most universities provide opportunities for mentorship in the form of advisors and contact with faculty members. However, it is up to you to take advantage of those mentorship opportunities. You can do that by raising questions and asking for information and advice that will help you be more successful. Most good mentors enjoy that role, but you can increase the likelihood that they will want to continue to mentor you by showing your appreciation.

I strongly recommend that you seek out opportunities for intense mentorship while in college. That usually involves working with faculty members either in their lab or in their area of scholarship. If this is done right, it will be a symbiotic relationship. You will benefit from their mentorship, and they will benefit from your energy and contributions to their work.

Mentorship should never be considered just an aspect of college. If you go on to graduate or professional schools, the role of mentors will increase because that is the primary way in which people are trained at that level. However, after you finish all your schooling and go on to your first job, you will continue to benefit from mentors. Mentors can provide both useful information and guidance and often emotional support. Over time, you will find yourself providing mentorship to other people, even while you are benefiting from the mentorship of others in your organization. That is the topic of the next chapter.

Chapter 13
Becoming a Mentor

I am betting that more than a few of you are surprised by this chapter. The whole point of this book is to prepare you to become an outstanding professional by using the resources and wisdom of mentors. However, the distinction of learning from a mentor and being a mentor to others is somewhat arbitrary. You learned earlier in this text that the worst way to get a good grade is to try to get a good grade; the best way to get a good grade is to learn the material well enough to teach it to someone else. The same concept applies to mentorship. If you look at the most successful people, they are often remarkable mentors to other people. Moreover, they often became mentors early in their career, even while they were learning from their own mentors.

It is not an accident that those people who utilize mentors most effectively often become outstanding mentors themselves. One may speculate that such people are simply "returning the favor." That may be true for some people, but as you will see in this chapter, the transition from being a mentee to being a mentor is often natural. Moreover, it is often the next step on the ladder of success. In this chapter, I will discuss this transition, why it is beneficial to the mentor, how to improve mentorship skills, and what being a mentor will return for the efforts.

Mentor/Mentee

The transition from mentee to mentor is not as dramatic as you may imagine. If you are like me, you may want to replace the word *mentee* with *protégé*. In fact, many dictionaries consider the word mentee clumsy at best, but you know what it means, and elegance is not always the most important factor in choosing your words.

Even some of the best protégés start out overwhelmed and not sure how to take advantage of the mentoring they are receiving. A consistent theme throughout this book is that we need to learn the

159

most effective ways of benefiting from the resources available to us. We also need to know what resources are available and how to access them. You may well have the resources of an outstanding mentor available to you right now, and you are not taking advantage of that opportunity. Even if you have a mentor, you need to learn to listen, experiment, and evaluate the effectiveness of whatever advice you get from him or her.

If you want to have outstanding mentors committed to helping you to succeed, you need to learn how to be an outstanding protégé. Every relationship is symbiotic, so if your mentor is providing valuable guidance and wisdom, it is your responsibility to return something of equal value. There are two primary ways in which you will return the favor of being mentored. The first is simply to be grateful and make it clear that you are grateful. A simple thank you will go a long way but coming back to a mentor and praising them for the wonderful advice is a powerful reinforcer. A hand-written note amplifies the reinforcement value of such feedback. The second way you return the favor to a mentor is to succeed. Mentors invest tremendous energy in your success, and they take great pride in everything you achieve. You will learn as you become a mentor yourself that your protégés are like sons and daughters. Mentors love to brag about their protégés; they love to follow their careers; they love to get together with their protégés and find out all the exciting things they are doing. It is a symbiotic interaction because protégés love to share their successes and relish the pride shown by the mentors.

The Value of Mentoring

There is no question that mentoring is an incredibly valuable service. Those people who are mentored do better in competitive situations than those who do not have the advice of a good mentor. The question in this chapter is what is the value of mentoring to the person doing the mentoring? In other words, why is it in your best interest to become a mentor?

The two elements most important in a good mentor are (1) wisdom and knowledge and (2) the ability to influence other people. Wisdom and knowledge are developed through careful observation and through working with effective people, who often are excellent mentors. But wisdom and knowledge require more. They require critical thinking about all the things we observe or are told. Think about it for a moment. No mentor is all knowing. Mentors make mistakes and sometimes offer advice that is not appropriate for us. If you want to use mentors effectively, listen to them carefully, but just as carefully, evaluate the appropriateness of the advice they give. You want to be sensitive to your own needs and desires so you can evaluate how well their advice is meeting those needs.

Since it is impossible to reliably pass on everything we know, if those people being mentored do not think critically, the imprecision of knowledge exchange will gradually decrease collective wisdom. Good ideas will gradually become bad ideas because of distortion in communicating them to others. But critical thinking corrects both misunderstandings and bad advice by always evaluating ideas against objective criteria, such as whether that strategy will work.

If you have benefited from being someone's protégé, if you have improved your performance by listening carefully to the advice of someone in the know, then you have wisdom that you did not have before, and you can pass on that wisdom to other people. Remember when we talked about learning earlier in this book? The best way to really learn material is to teach it to other people. Ideas we thought we knew well suddenly become less clear when we try to explain them to someone else. That is a valuable signal; it tells us that we do not know the ideas as well as we thought. With that information, we can think more about the material, ask knowledgeable people the right questions to clarify our understanding, and then verify that we truly understand it because we can explain it effectively to other people. Why do you want to mentor other people? Because by mentoring other people, you will reinforce all that you have learned from the mentors in your life. A nice side effect is that you will help talented and hardworking people to be more successful, and they will appreciate you for it.

I mentioned earlier that wisdom and knowledge are only one of two elements needed to be an effective mentor. To be an effective mentor, you also need to be skilled at influencing people. After all, if you give people good advice and they ignore you, you certainly cannot say that you have been an effective mentor. Advice usually translates into something that should be done, and when people must do something, it requires work. People do not work at things they do not believe in. Mentors often give excellent advice to individuals who have talent and potential, but they also give those individuals something even more important. They give them the message that someone believes in them and believes they have the potential to be outstanding. Why else would someone take time out of their busy schedule to encourage and advise the person?

Effectively recruiting protégés and mentoring them so that their performance increases is the ultimate behavioral evidence of your own wisdom, knowledge, and interpersonal leadership skills. Every organization needs talented people, and almost every organization has fewer talented people than they would like. If you are one of those talented people, you will be rewarded for that talent and hard work. If you are one of those talented people who can also bring out the talent in other individuals (i.e., mentor them), then you are even more valuable. The best reason for making the transition from being someone who is being mentored to someone who is capable of mentoring others is that it is a great way to advance your own career. There is another reason that I personally find important. It feels good to help others believe in themselves and be successful at a level they may never have been able to reach without your help.

Developing Mentoring Skills

No one starts out as an elite mentor. You start out giving simple advice to the people around you. Those people may be friends, coworkers, or people you are helping as part of your job. In these early encounters, you will walk a fine line between being helpful and being bossy or a know-it-all. If people ask you a question, giving them a quick and accurate answer is a great start. If you see them struggling with a problem, gently asking if you can help will often elicit their invitation for you to help them (i.e., to mentor them). You can provide help in multiple ways. Sometimes, just listening to their concerns provides the emotional support to help them get back on track. Other times, you may provide advice on actions that can help them make things work better.

You need to learn to include encouragement and frequent praise to promote the effort needed to be successful. In the process, you refine your abilities to influence people, to manage major projects, and to build the goodwill of those individuals under your authority. That last phrase may be somewhat disconcerting to you. You probably think of authority as being something that involves being the boss and signing the checks. That certainly is authority, but it is not the only kind of authority. If you are working on a group project in an undergraduate class, and in the discussion, you ask the right questions about how to proceed, you have established your authority based on your clear thinking about the problem faced jointly by the group. You can take it a step further by reinforcing group members that step up with their own ideas or agree to take primary responsibility for some aspect of the project. Suddenly, you have taken on a leadership role, not by claiming it, but rather by demonstrating the actions of a leader.

Most of us have had bosses who simply could not command authority even though they technically had authority. If they could hire and fire people, then they clearly had authority. If you want to be a great mentor, you need to recognize that your authority rests much more on your ability to do the job and work with the people around you than your job title. Think about some of the teachers you have had. In college, virtually every one of them had an advanced degree and were being paid to be an instructor. But think about the teachers you absolutely trusted, the ones that changed the way you thought about things, the ones who encouraged you to go beyond the content of the course. They had authority. They had much more authority than those teachers who could not inspire anyone even though they had the same position and the same responsibility for assigning grades. If you wanted to ask for advice,

163

you would be far more likely to approach one of those outstanding teachers rather than a teacher for whom you had little respect.

So how can college instructors develop authority in the classroom? Well, first, they must know what they are talking about. Most college students are smart; they recognize when someone is faking it. Since no one knows everything, one way of building a reputation for being a good scholar is to recognize and acknowledge the limits of your knowledge. If a student asks a question and you do not know the answer, a good response may be, "That's a great question. I never thought about that question before, and I am not sure what the answer is. Let's think about the likely answer given what we already know about the topic." With this response, the instructor is acknowledging the good work of the student first. Nothing improves a course more than students who ask great questions. The instructor is also acknowledging his or her limits and modeling how one would start the process of answering such a good question. Perhaps the answer will come out of the discussion, but if it does not, the instructor can model the process of digging deeper into a good question by researching the question and bringing answers back to the class later.

Crammed into the previous paragraph is a ton of information about styles that work well for establishing one's authority. The example above is certainly not the only way of doing it, but the style tends to be appreciated by students and rewarded in the course evaluations. I hope you have never had an instructor who routinely insulted students for asking questions. That instructor may be knowledgeable but certainly will never be able to command authority. There is no shortcut to knowing the material. I have always thought that as a professor, I was paid to learn and that I taught as a secondary value of my learning. My job was to be on the cutting edge so I could help students be on the cutting edge. But you need to pair that information with the social skills to truly influence those people you have authority over.

There is a principal that is sometimes overlooked when developing any professional skill. That principle is feedback. If you make a diagnosis, suggest a strategy for solving a problem, or mentor someone, you need feedback on whether you were correct

164

if you want to improve. Doctors who discover that their diagnoses were incorrect need to figure out where they went wrong so they can get it right the next time. If your strategy for solving an engineering problem proves to be inadequate, you should be motivated to figure out how you blew it. The fields that have advanced most rapidly are the ones that systematically demand such feedback (Meehl, 1973).

If you want to be an outstanding mentor, be sure to follow up with each of your protégés to see how they are doing and what advice has been most effective. It is also important to find out what advice was ineffective. That can be difficult because it is easy to be defensive when hearing about things that we did not do well, but the best professionals learn to listen to such feedback and improve their performance as a result. This strategy not only works for improving your mentorship but also for improving every aspect of your professional work.

Mentorship as an Asset

Having good grades or high scores on entrance exams is a real asset if you are considering graduate school. Having a history of being an effective mentor is also a real asset. The most effective leaders are also good mentors. As a graduate student, you will likely be mentored by a faculty member while you are simultaneously mentoring other students. You want to offer concrete evidence that you are already an effective mentor in your application package for graduate school. That evidence may be a letter of recommendation from someone who worked closely with you and observed you mentoring others. It may be a job that involved mentoring, such as being an academic tutor. Remember what I have said repeatedly: claiming a skill is one thing, but without evidence to support the claim, your claim carries little weight. When you finally earn an advanced degree, evidence of your skill as a mentor is even more important in getting you a great first job.

Mentoring the Right People

As a college student, many of the students you will be mentoring will be selected for you. They may be someone you are training to do specific tasks in a lab or office. They may be people you are tutoring or training in specific skills, such as data analysis, library skills, or writing. Every chance to mentor someone should be used as a learning opportunity. Remember that it is possible to spend two hours reading and not remember a single thing you read? That happens because reading is so automatic that we do not have to think to do it, but if we want to learn, we must be actively thinking. If you want to develop your mentorship skills, you must focus on what you are doing as a mentor and what effect it is having.

As your career develops, you will have increasingly more control over your professional life, including who you will be mentoring. Mentoring requires energy, and you should look on that energy as a resource to invest. If you have discretionary money, you will likely look for a way to invest that money so it will grow or provide you with a satisfying experience. Every resource you have, including money, is a resource that should be invested with an eye to how much and when it will provide a return. Of course, we cannot predict the stock market, so we may make financial investments that fail. In the same way, we will sometimes agree to make an investment in someone by providing mentorship and will discover that it was not a wise investment. However, even those difficult situations can provide valuable life lessons, such as patience, how to be direct, and when to refer a person to someone else.

What makes an investment in mentoring a wise investment? There is no single answer to this question. Sometimes, the mentoring will produce skills and attitudes that promote our work in addition to being valuable to the person being mentored. Sometimes, the successful mentoring of an individual can dramatically enhance your reputation. You will be amazed at how often professionals observe a rising star and want to know who had a role in shaping these individuals. Finally, sometimes the investment is repaid almost immediately by the positive feelings associated with being a part of that relationship. In my experience, this last item has been powerful because most of the people I have mentored were a delight to mentor. However, such immediate rewards for mentoring are not universal. I must admit that I have had a couple of students that I mentored who were constant challenges and rarely rewarding, but who eventually blossomed. They certainly were not fun to mentor, but I am nonetheless proud of my influence on them.

You may wonder why you should worry about who you choose to mentor. If you had unlimited energy, there would be no reason to be concerned. However, you do not have unlimited energy, and any energy that you focus on one task will necessarily prevent you from focusing on another task. Frankly, I feel a little silly writing this paragraph because I have always been notoriously bad at saying no to things. Several decades ago, I spent a lot of money having a small plaque made up to set on my desk that said, "If you say yes to one thing, you will have to say no to something else." I would like to tell you that that plaque has worked; actually, it has helped, but I still tend to say yes far too often. But even though I may not be very good at saying no, I encourage you to be better at it. So carefully choose the people you honor with your mentorship and invest your time and energy into making the world a better place by making them better professionals.

Chapter Summary

Much of this book focused on how to use mentors to prepare for professional careers and the advanced education required for many of those careers. That information is important, but it is also important for you to realize that one of the defining characteristics of professionals is that they will be mentoring other professionals. Therefore, you want to learn from your mentors, not only how to be more competitive now, but also how to be a more effective mentor to others.

Being an effective mentor is a highly marketable asset. It is something that admissions committees look for when selecting graduate students or students for professional programs. It is one of those skills that do not show up on your transcript but can show up on your résumé, in your personal statement, or in the letters of recommendation that support your application to graduate/professional school or for a job. To be an effective mentor, you need to know the topic area well, but you also need to be able to sell your protégés on strategies for success. Since each person is different, the strategies used to mentor individuals are likely to be different as well. The best mentors are amazingly flexible at adjusting their strategy depending on who they are mentoring.

Chapter 14
Building a Support System

These last two chapters may seem out of place. Most of this book has focused on things you can do to be more successful in college, graduate/professional school, and your career. Each of the skills and attitudes we talked about will indeed give you an edge in competing with others. What we have not talked about until now is how to take care of yourself so you have the energy and resilience needed to continue to compete month after month and year after year.

In this chapter, we will talk about importance of your support system. All of us need support, and the idea that needing support is a sign of weakness is crazy. The harder you work and the more competitive you are, the more you will be faced with emotional challenges that could be overwhelming without the support of others. Support is a two-way street. If you want to be confident that there are people willing to provide support when you need it, you will need to provide support to them when they need it.

Inevitable Stressors

The pessimistic claim, "Life is a bitch, and then you die," may not be entirely false, but it is certainly an overstatement. It leaves out all the wonderful things that make life worthwhile. However, it does capture the fact that most random events are negative. It is true that sometimes life can be a bitch. It is also true that sometimes we do everything right and it still does not work out the way we would like. Those days can feel like an emotional gut punch. There may be things you can do that will help you recover from or avoid the costly consequences of such events. However, it is unlikely that you can plan well enough to avoid these bad days completely.

Although stressful events are inevitable, there are things you can do to reduce their consequences. Setbacks often have their impact because we do not have sufficient time or resources to recover. For example, something goes wrong when we are up against a deadline. Sometimes, it seems like the world knows we are up against a deadline and decides to make life miserable for us by giving us a cold, having our computer lock up, or giving us a headache from hell. These things do seem to come at the worst times, although there is a perfectly reasonable alternative hypothesis. It could be that the bad cold that makes it hard for us to think is more stressful because we have something important due tomorrow. If that same important project was due in a week, that serious cold would have just been a frustrating hassle instead of an overwhelming stressor.

The above examples give us one of the most effective ways to reduce the impact of the inevitable hassles of life. If you consistently plan to have everything run smoothly so you complete all required tasks on the day they are due, buckle up for a rough ride. It is rare that everything in life runs smoothly; you should expect that things will go wrong because they often do. The more you build in time to recover from such hassles, the less disruptive those hassles will be. In college, for example, if you have a paper due on Monday, it would be a great idea to finish it on Friday. If you get a cold or your computer goes on strike, you still have plenty of time to meet the Monday deadline. If everything goes right and you finish on Friday, you can have a relaxing weekend and have time on Sunday afternoon to do one quick revision to significantly improve your paper.

Earlier, I talked about the excellent advice that I got from the professor I studied with in graduate school. He told me that to plan a project of any significance, I should list every possible task involved in that project and the maximum amount of time it should take. He then told me that if I doubled that amount, I would still be overly optimistic but at least in the ballpark. I thought he was kidding; it turned out to be the best advice I ever received. The truth is it always takes longer than we expect to do just about anything. It is true when we are in college; it is true when we are in graduate or professional school; it will be true your entire life. In time, you will get better at estimating how long tasks will take because the rule described above will be incorporated into your thinking. Optimism is a wonderful trait in a professional. However, unreasonable optimism can make your life miserable because you will misjudge what is possible and therefore will put yourself into impossible situations.

The impact of inevitable stressors in your life can also be reduced if you think in terms of having a plan B in place before it is desperately needed. Let me give you an example that is probably relevant right now and certainly will be relevant throughout your professional life. We can live without computers, but I certainly do not want to. I could have written this book on a typewriter or with a pen and paper, but the computer made things much easier. For example, I am dictating this paragraph and will polish it later without having to retype it. But our reliance on computers for writing papers or books makes us vulnerable unless we have taken steps to reduce that vulnerability. How do we reduce such vulnerability?

When I dictate or type on my computer, it shows up on the screen. At least initially, that is the only place that it shows up. But my word processor is set to automatically save what I am doing every five minutes. If I lose power, I only lose five minutes of work. I have another backup in place if I lose power; I have a battery that will run my computer long enough for me to safely close out everything before I shut down. I also have yet another backup system that automatically transfers a copy of everything saved on my computer into the cloud. It is a program called Dropbox, and it is free if the amount you want to save in the cloud is not too large. I pay a little extra so I can save everything. Moreover, Dropbox also syncs everything I have saved on every computer I work on. Dropbox is only one of several products that provide both backup and syncing of work between computers. I was motivated to put all these backups into place because I have had bad things happen to me. If you are lucky enough that your computer hard drive has never crashed, I hate to tell you that it will happen at some point. Have I had computer problems since I put all of this in place? Of course I have! But those problems were trivial because each of these plan Bs allowed for an easy and quick recovery.

Since I initially wrote the above paragraph, I purchased a new computer that replaces the mechanical hard drive with a more reliable memory system. Will that eliminate hard drive crashes? Yes, because there is no hard drive. Will the system never fail? I doubt it, but I do suspect that it will reduce the failure rate. This new purchase is just one more example of a modification of plans to reduce the chances of a serious setback.

Sources of Support

Before we cover sources of support, I want to make a distinction between two types of support. One type gives you practical and professional support to recover from a setback; the other type gives you emotional support to bounce back from a setback.

Professional Support

Most people think of sources of support as family and friends. These people are indeed a very important source of support. In general, however, the support they provide is emotional. They listen to us when we are down and give us encouragement. Such support is critical at times, and I will cover it later in this section. However, I want to start with a different kind of support. I am going to call this type of support *professional support*. This support includes people who can help us solve the problems rather than help us to deal with the frustration associated with the problems.

These sources of professional support will vary depending upon your stage in life. In college, your primary sources of professional support would be your advisor, the chair and the administrative assistant for your major department, the financial aid officer, the health clinic for students, the library and its professional librarians, and the instructors in each of your courses.

Most colleges or universities have departments that are set up for the sole purpose of providing professional support. For example, every university will have an IT department that provides professional support to both faculty and students. That department can help you set up your computer and often will provide free software to help students function more effectively in college. If you are having a problem with your computer, this department can help you track down the problem and solve it.

It is common for a university to include both a writing and a math center because these are often areas in which students need to improve their skills, and the instructors in their courses do not have time to provide the necessary instruction. Many universities also include tutorial services organized into a single center. The tutorials may focus on selected classes, but sometimes they focus on general topics like study skills. These are all valuable sources of support for the college student. You are paying for these programs with your tuition. They are not a gift; they are a resource opportunity for you to use.

We previously talked about the importance of mentors. You will not find a mentor center at your university. Instead, you develop relationships with mentors by seeking them out and taking advantage of the information and advice that they can offer. These are clearly professional support systems, and they may be the most important source of professional support you will receive during your college career. Because we have talked at length about mentors, I will not repeat that information in this chapter.

Professional support systems help us minimize problems when they occur and prevent problems by anticipating them and either building the skills to avoid them or preparing the resources that will help us recover when those problems occur. To have these resources available, you need to know what they are and how to access them. Many universities have recognized that it can be a challenge to find the right resource person when you need support. Consequently, the university may have set up a triage program that essentially points students in the right direction when they need professional support. At the very least, if such a program exists on your campus, make sure you know where it is and how to contact it.

Many professional support services are best used to prevent problems. It may be a great idea, for example, to take one or more of the library orientation programs. These programs will give you the skills to use the library effectively when you need it later in your college career. Many people assume that a writing center is only for those people who need remedial training in writing. It is certainly a valuable source of professional support for those people, but it can be an equally valuable professional support for those strong students who will end up getting advanced degrees. Improving one's writing always strengthens the image one presents to others. Tutoring can help students who are having difficulty learning, but it can also help strong students who want to truly understand the material at a higher level.

Emotional Support

When faced with a difficult professional challenge, your first goal should be to overcome the difficulty. It would be nice if you could overcome all difficulties, but that is not the real world. In the real world, sometimes you fail. Failure is difficult, it is demoralizing, and it can rob us of the optimism we need to keep trying. But as human beings, we can utilize the support of others to get through such difficult times.

Support comes in many forms. Sometimes, it is as simple as your parents giving you money to cover unexpected expenses. Sometimes, it is just having someone who cares enough about you to listen to your frustrations and offer their condolences. Sometimes, it is just a hug; it is amazing the power of a simple hug. The key to getting emotional support is having friends and family available for such support. There is a second key that is often overlooked. Even if you have the kind of support system that will get you through difficult times, you need to tell those people when you need their support. If your parents, siblings, friends, or spouse do not know how much you are hurting, they are not likely to know that you need them to be supportive.

Building that Support Network

If we are lucky, we come with a built-in support network: our family. I am not naïve enough to think that families always get along or that they always love one another, but often they do love one another despite constant fighting. Even when they do not get along, families may be willing to be there because of that love. If you are just starting college, you may be at an age at which your relationship with your parents is strained. That is normal, and it says nothing about how much your parents love you or, for that matter, how much you love them. You need not tell your parents everything that is going on in your life. After all, you are an adult and living your own life. Just do not shut them out entirely from your life. Tell them about some of the good things happening to you, such as the course that has really caught your attention. Tell them about some of the bad things that happened to you, such as the friend who disappointed you. Sharing such things keeps the channels of communication open for those times when you truly need the support of your parents.

The previous paragraph may have been painful for you if you do not have the kind of supportive parents I am describing. I consider myself lucky because I did have great parents, and they were supportive when I needed their support. But as a clinical psychologist running the training clinic for PhD clinical psychology students, I often learned about clients who did not have the luxury of supportive families. When I did, I often called my parents just to say thank you for who they were and for the love and support they had given me. They were always modest, saying something like, "We were just doing our job." I bring this up because my simple thank you had an enormous impact on my parents. I wish I had had the insight earlier in my life to recognize how important their support was. I wish I had thought to say, "Thank you for all your support. I know that we do not always agree, but I love you and I know you love me." If you show more maturity than I did when I was younger and say something to that effect, you will reinforce the strongest of loving bonds.

If you have siblings, one or more of them may be wonderful sources of support. You may be more comfortable sharing things of a personal nature with your siblings than with your parents. But not everyone has siblings, and even if you do have siblings, there is no guarantee you will have a close supportive relationship with them. However, you can nurture such a relationship by regularly sharing and eagerly listening when they want to share.

Most of us get our support primarily from friends. The word *friend* is overused these days. Many people have hundreds of "friends" on Facebook or other online forums. That is not what I am talking about here. The kind of friends who can give us support when we truly need it are rare and require extensive time for nurturing. It is unlikely that you would need more than one hand to count these special friends. It takes time and shared experiences to build that kind of supportive relationship. Sometimes, all that energy is for naught because close friends move away or get busy with other things or other people in their life, and you drift apart. On the other hand, some of these relationships can remain strong despite living a thousand or more miles apart and rarely seeing one another.

The effort that it takes to maintain these close relationships is a great investment. Make it a point to connect on a regular basis. If you work together or engage in special activities together, that will be easy. If you do not, find things you can do that fit your schedules and your shared interests. You may play golf together, go to garage sales together, or have breakfast once a week. If you select the activity carefully, you will both enjoy the time together and will continue to cement a relationship. You can also use the time to get that everyday kind of support that comes with talking to someone who is a good friend.

When we talk about building a support network, most people immediately think in terms of family and friends, and that has been our focus so far in this section. But we can get support from other places, and how easily we can get the support from those places will depend on how well we have nurtured those supports. For example, a college student may well get support from his or her advisor or from specific teachers. These people will often provide the support simply because it is part of their job. However, it is possible to nurture supportive relationships with people who normally are at a much higher level than you. If you work for a faculty member or take several classes from that faculty member, you can build a relationship by showing your interest in them and their work. A teacher who truly enjoys having you in class because you truly enjoy the class is far more likely to want to reach out and help you if you find yourself in a difficult situation. If you go on to graduate school, you will likely develop a strong mentorship relationship with a faculty member who is responsible for your graduate training. That relationship can develop into a lifelong friendship under the right circumstances and can certainly be a valuable source of support during what is usually a challenging time in your life. Your peers in graduate or professional school will also be an incredible source of support, and the relationships you form with your peers will likely last a lifetime.

Rarely do people think of their boss as a source of support, and I believe that is a strategic mistake. By its very nature, the relationship between a boss and an employee should be naturally symbiotic. The boss depends on the quality work of employees and wants to motivate those employees to improve the quality of their work. Employees want to be appreciated and rewarded for the work they do. If you are a good and loyal employee, and if you respect and follow your boss's wishes, your boss will want to do everything in his or her power to keep you. That means that if you are suffering a personal trauma, such as a health problem with one of your family members, the boss has an incentive to provide support to reward your hard work and loyalty.

I want to address one last issue associated with support in the workplace. Things may change in the workplace because a coworker suddenly becomes your boss or vice versa. The dynamics of the relationship change when someone gets promoted and peers are now in a boss/employee relationship. It does not necessarily mean that the supportive relationship you had with that person will end, but almost certainly it means it will change. There are no rules on how to deal with such relationship changes, and frankly, some people handle such relationship changes badly. But just as I have argued that a boss/employee relationship can be supportive, a coworker relationship that turns into a boss/employee relationship can evolve into a different type of supportive situation.

Dealing with Overwhelming Challenges

It is my sincere hope that you will never have to deal with the kind of overwhelming challenge that may exceed your ability to cope. However, such challenges may indeed be part of your future. What am I talking about? It may be a severe setback to your career, such as losing your job in a hostile takeover or, worse, being fired because you made a foolish mistake. It may be the breakup of a critical relationship, such as with your spouse or with a close friend. It may be the loss of a child; we expect that we will bury our parents, but we are rarely emotionally prepared to bury our children. Whatever the overwhelming challenge is, its effects can be devastating unless we take rapid and effective action.

Since it is unpredictable how and when a tragedy may affect us, it is difficult to be prepared for everything that may happen. Having good sources of general support from family, from friends, from coworkers, and from spiritual advisors will give us the range of resources to draw on when faced with a tragedy. Unfortunately, many professionals have been led to believe that they must have complete control of their emotions to be effective. That may work most of the time, but it is rarely effective when faced with tragic circumstances. Even if one could control their emotions when faced with tragedy—that is, to cope by becoming emotionally numb—the cost is too high a price to pay.

The key when facing a tragedy is to seek help early and accept help when it is offered. Now, some people are more helpful than others, so if you have a choice, rely on those individuals who are generally more effective at providing support. When faced with a tragedy, the last thing you need is a high-maintenance individual as your source of support. Everyone needs support, and the most effective support is human. Alcohol and drugs can feel like support when one is completely overwhelmed, but the long-term negative effects far outweigh any advantage of relying on these methods.

One of the most important things to remember when faced with a tragedy is that you are stronger as a group then you are individually. We tend to idealize independence in our culture and contrast it with dependence, which we view as weakness. But the strength of human beings is that they are stronger together than individually, and the most adapted human beings are those who provide support for others when needed and benefit from the support of others when they need it. That combination is called *interdependence*. You need to do some personal cognitive therapy if you find yourself saying that your response to tragedy is a sign of weakness. It is not! It is a sign of being human, and you want to use the strengths of human beings to get you through the worst of times.

Chapter Summary

Sometimes it appears that certain people are blessed in that they never experience serious setbacks in their professional or personal lives. That is an illusion. It may appear that way because those individuals have created and nurtured a support system that buffers them from the same setbacks everyone experiences. Stress is inevitable, but with the proper planning, one can bounce back quickly from many predictable problems. The trick is to recognize the likelihood of those setbacks and have one or more plans ready to address a problem once it occurs.

There are several methods to obtain the kind of support we will all need at one time or another. Many sources of support, called *professional support*, are focused on solving a problem or mitigating the negative impact of a problem when it occurs. These sources of support can also involve structuring things to avoid some of the setbacks that are part of life. But not all problems can be solved, and many setbacks have strong emotional consequences. In those situations, we need the emotional support of family and friends. If we have taken the time and invested the energy to build those relationships, they will be there to get us through the most difficult of times.

Chapter 15
Balance: The Key to Long-Term Success

Well, you have made it this far, and hopefully in the process you have learned things that will be helpful. The entire point of this book is to give you information early enough that it will make you more competitive in those critical early years of your career, including your college career. This book is only one source of information. As you learned, mentors at various stages of your career can be enormously helpful in guiding you to make good decisions.

So what else is there? Information only buys you so much. It can reduce the likelihood of mistakes that will derail your progress. It can help you make decisions early enough to supercharge your career. What it cannot do is advance your progress. Only you can do that. There is no substitute for hard work, responsible action, and continual learning if you want to be successful. There will be good days, and there will be days that are challenging. And, unfortunately, there will be days that seem impossible. We only have so much energy, and there will be days in which that energy is totally spent.

No one has an unlimited source of energy. No one has unlimited resilience, which allows us to bounce back from any setback. No one has unlimited optimism that fuels effort even on the worst of days. The truth is that we need to refuel our energy on a regular basis if we want to be successful. We need the strength provided by social relationships to bounce back from difficult situations. We need the wisdom and support of others to provide a sense of optimism that is tempered with realism. In this final chapter, I will be talking about the importance of structuring your life in a way that allows you not only to be successful but also to enjoy your life.

Why Do We Need Balance?

I have often pondered the words of Massachusetts senator Paul Tsongas (1984), who once ran for president of the United States. A talented individual who was respected by his peers on both sides of the aisle, Tsongas had a strong sense of the meaning of life. He had survived cancer before he decided to run for president. Had he won the presidency, he would not have survived his first term because the cancer returned and took his life. The words he wrote that had such an impact on me were, "When you are on your deathbed, you almost never wish you had spent more time at the office."

Paul Tsongas was certainly not the only person to verbalize such a sentiment, and his wording may not be better than the wording offered by other people. It may simply be that I read his words at a critical time in my life. Whatever the reason, his words had an impact on me; they helped me to change my life, and I have tried to share his wisdom in various ways with my students and friends.

Perhaps a less inspirational quote, which we discussed earlier, is, "Life sucks and then you die." The original source of this quotation is unclear, and it appears to have been voiced by many people over the years. I suspect some of you may have smiled as you read that quote, suspecting that there is a kernel of truth in it. Life is difficult, and if you want to be successful, you can expect that there will be many roadblocks. The focus of this book has been on trying to avoid roadblocks by making good decisions early enough to carry you through. It is my sincere hope that you will avoid some roadblocks, but I am confident in predicting that you will not avoid all of them.

What Is Balance?

Balance is a difficult concept to define, but most of us have a sense of what it means. We all recognize that things will happen in life that will knock us off balance. A few years back a popular bumper sticker, which was immortalized in the movie Forrest Gump, summed it up well: "Shit Happens!" Not only does it happen, but also it happens more often than we would like, and it is guaranteed to happen to all of us at one time or another. When it does, we need to adjust course or utilize the available resources to regain our balance and continue to make progress.

The natural response when such things happen is emotional. We are angry, frustrated, discouraged, and overwhelmed. It knocks us off balance, which is to say that we feel unsteady and uncertain about how to proceed. Often, we are uncertain because there is no obvious way to proceed. Consequently, we feel stuck, lost, and even abandoned. The good thing is that when shit happens to us, it usually affects just one part of our life. For example, we may experience a serious setback in our job, a major problem in our relationships, or a personal crisis of confidence. Those are real and disruptive, but they are more disruptive when all our self-esteem comes from that one area in which we are experiencing the setback.

The ultimate source of balance is to have more than one area of your life that gives you satisfaction and support. Most of us divide our lives into domains, such as work, family, friends, and recreation. These domains are neither mutually exclusive nor exhaustive. For example, it is entirely possible that your recreational life will overlap both your family and friends, and there may be a critical domain in your life other than the ones listed here (an important hobby, quiet time, etc.). But if you have multiple domains that give you satisfaction, you can fall back on another when you experience a setback in a particular domain. If you lose your job, you can focus on how important your family is to you. If your marriage breaks up, you can focus on work or friends. Eventually, you must address the problem area, but for a time, the other areas of importance can provide solace. You will find another job or will either repair your marriage or find another relationship. But until those adjustments can be made, you still have a source of meaning in your life.

What Resources Provide Balance?

Once you accept that you will be knocked off balance during your life, the central question becomes how you recover your balance. Although there is no single answer to this question, there is a principle that can guide your decisions now and prepare you for such events. Those who recover their balance most quickly following negative events have anticipated potential negative events and accumulated necessary resources to deal with them.

Some planning is simple, such as planning for financial setbacks. Purchasing insurance against potential risks can dramatically reduce the financial impact of such events. If your home is severely damaged in a storm, your place of business is broken into and expensive equipment is stolen, or your car is involved in a serious accident, the financial consequences of these events can be covered by the insurance. An alternative way to prepare for financial setbacks is to create a savings account, which has the advantage of being able to cover almost any financial setback. If you lose your job because the company you work for goes bankrupt, you can live off your savings while you look for a new job. You can even combine these two strategies. If you have money in savings, you can afford a large deductible on your insurance policies, which will dramatically decrease the cost of those insurance policies. The deductible is the amount you must pay before the insurance kicks in. If the cost of fixing your car after an accident is $7,000 and you have a $2,000 deductible, you will pay the first $2,000, and the insurance company will pay the rest.

Financial setbacks are the easiest to address of the various crises that one can face, although frankly, early in your career, you may not have the financial resources needed to reduce these risks completely. If you lose your job, there is certainly a financial consequence, and those consequences will be severe if you have no financial resources to tide you over until you get another job. However, the loss of income may be the least significant problem associated with losing your job. Depending on the reason for losing the job, there is likely to be a significant emotional impact that will affect you for months or years. Depending on the situation, finding a new position may take time, and that time will take a toll on your self-confidence and your competitiveness for other positions. The economy is volatile and changing rapidly, and as a corollary, the trajectory of jobs is increasingly volatile. I sincerely hope that you will never face a situation where your job is eliminated, but it would be wise for you to plan on that happening simply because it is likely, given how rapidly things are changing today. You may not be given a pink slip at 4:00 PM on a Friday, but you may be working for a company that is rapidly moving toward bankruptcy. You may still technically have a job, but if you do not move on soon, you likely will be moving on while collecting unemployment.

There are several things that one may do to plan for a possible job loss. One is to build a savings account to handle the financial aspect. A second is to constantly develop new skills that would make you valuable to your current company or to other companies if your current job were to be eliminated. A third is to develop contacts with people in the industry so that if you need to look for a new job, you will have people who can help you find a suitable position. Finally, it is always helpful to have your curriculum vitae or résumé up-to-date and to have an active LinkedIn account. All these approaches sound good, but you may be asking the central question of how you deal with the emotional devastation of losing your job.

Losing your job is only one of many devastating events that may be part of your life. Having a relationship breakup, having a friend or family member die, failing at something that was important for you, or experiencing a severe setback in some aspect of your life will always have emotional repercussions. If most of our life is going well, we may be able to ride out these inevitable setbacks reasonably well. But the single most important thing that will buffer us through these setbacks are strong emotional connections with other people.

We are stronger as a group than we are individually. When we are a team, we can support one another and rally one another. Sometimes, we need a hug, and that is not a sign of weakness. Sometimes other people need hugs, and we can be there for them. That is a good symbiotic relationship. You must build and nourish such relationships throughout your life to have the sources of support to get through those difficult times.

Supportive relationships begin with family. I know that not every family is supportive and not every family member is a best friend. Still, family is important for most of us and is the primary source of support during the most difficult times. But family is not enough. We need friends, and by friends I do not mean the people who have "friended" us on Facebook or on LinkedIn. For many people, their church is a significant source of supportive individuals. For others, it may be service organizations or clubs built around specific activities (e.g., golf, gardening, reading, hunting, etc.). These are places in which you may have contacts, but very few of those contacts become true friends. When we are talking about support, we are talking about making and cultivating these true friendships.

What is a true friendship, and what does it take? A true friendship is a symbiotic relationship in which people share information, activities, support, and enjoyment in good times and sorrow in bad times. It is rare to have more than half a dozen such true friendships because maintaining such friendships requires significant energy and effort. But the expenditure of energy is well worth it because these are the people that will get us through the most difficult times. Having other friends and people you enjoy doing things with is great, and these people will help to make life worthwhile and enjoyable. But those unique people who are, to use current terminology, our BFFs (best friends forever) should always be a priority for us.

How Do We Recover When Knocked Off Balance?

There are many things you can do to create a balance in your life and thus enable yourself to deal with the inevitable ups and downs of life. There is probably nothing that you can do that will buffer you from all the challenges of life, and therefore you can expect that you will be knocked off balance periodically. The people we call winners are not people who win all the time; they are the people who come back most quickly from losses. So, do what you can to create a balance in your life, but realize that you will get knocked down and you need to know how to get back up.

Supportive family and friends are incredibly important when we are down, but there will be times when we need more expertise than our friends can offer. That expertise falls into several categories. Some professionals can help us with medical or emotional problems, giving us the information and support we need to overcome these problems. Other professionals can give us the financial, educational, or occupational information, support, and direction to address specific setbacks. The wise individual takes the time to find such people before a crisis develops. The most successful people routinely surround themselves with experts that provide both support and advice in areas outside of their own expertise. It is important to remember that we are judged by what we achieve and how we achieve it, not by whether we achieve it solely through our own effort.

Chapter Summary

The theme of this book is that success in our careers can be heavily influenced by decisions we make in college and beyond, and we will make better decisions if we understand how the game is played. I know that life is more than a game, but sometimes appreciating that there are rules and expectations that are remarkably game-like will help us be more successful. Being successful is not a binary state in which we are either successful or not successful. Even the most successful people will fail occasionally. To use a sports analogy, the best batters in the history of baseball only got a hit about 40 percent of the time. The rest of the time, they failed to get a hit.

In this final chapter, I focused on building the life supports that allow us to recover from the inevitable failures in life. That is as important to your career success as your educational background, your choice of mentors, and the professional goals you set. However, the kind of supports talked about in this chapter are far more important than just buffers against career setbacks. They are often the most important things in life.

Postscript

It is my sincere hope that the information in this book will help you be more successful in whatever career direction you choose. However, I want you to enjoy your success in the context of a life that is personally satisfying, emotionally enriching, and personally meaningful, so your career success is only one piece of a life well lived.

I hope that the advice is helpful, but I also hope that you will get more than good advice from this book. If you have gotten this far in this book, you are clearly a serious student. You are likely to be successful, and your performance will give you options in life. But you will also expect a lot of yourself—sometimes too much. You will make mistakes and have setbacks. It happens to everyone, and it is hard not to take it personally. You are not a failure if you fail at something. It only means you are human. I know from personal experience that my character traits that tend to be praised by others are not always beneficial. Sometimes, I am my own worst enemy, and I suspect that many of you may be in the same boat.

Take a moment right now to praise yourself for investing the time and energy to read this book. You need to pat yourself on the back occasionally. In fact, make it a point to pat yourself on the back routinely. When things go wrong and you fail at something, focus on how to do it better rather than on the fact that you failed. And then, pat yourself on the back for both your attitude and your actions. I am not worried that you will suddenly drop all your high standards. Be proud of those standards but give yourself permission to be human. It is a delicate balance, and I would like to tell you that I have maintained that balance throughout my own personal and professional lives. But if I did, that would be a lie.

Finally, I want to wish you the best in your college career and beyond. Becoming a professional and maintaining high professional standards throughout your career can be very

Michael Raulin

satisfying. You can make a real difference in the world, but you will find that you make that difference one person at a time.

Glossary

associations: Links between ideas that help us to organize information in our memories. Associations can often trigger memories that appear initially to be outside of our reach.

attribution: An interpretation of the reason for events occurring. Attributions can either increase or decrease a person's risk for developing depression after experiencing one or more personal failures.

deliberate practice: Practice conducted under a high level of concentration in which the person exerts considerable effort to refine the behavior to the highest level of performance.

eidetic memory: The ability to remember specific details flawlessly after a single exposure to the material. Often called a photographic memory, someone with an eidetic memory can literally read the pages of a book from their memory as if a photograph of those pages is in front of the person.

elaborative rehearsal: Making a conscious effort to remember something so that you can recall it later. Elaborative rehearsal often involves relating the new material that you are trying to remember to other material that you already know.

fixed mindset: The idea that one has a fixed level of ability, such as a fixed intelligence, and that little can be done to increase that ability. In a fixed mindset, people avoid engaging in challenging new situations because there is a high likelihood of failure as one tries to master new things. A fixed mindset person would interpret that failure as evidence that the person has a low level of native ability.

flipped classroom: A teaching style in which instructors use classroom time to test the understanding of students rather than lecture about the material. Students are expected to read the book and listen to recorded lectures in advance so that they have some idea of the material. The class is then devoted to the process of testing whether students can output what they have learned instead of simply providing input of the material.

global versus specific attributions: Global attributions for failure assume that the cause of the failure applies to most or all other situations. Consequently, one can expect to fail at almost everything. In contrast, specific attributions for failure apply only to a single situation and thus we have no reason to expect general failure at everything.

growth mindset: The idea that one's abilities can be modified with practice, training, and hard work. In a growth mindset, one expects failures to occur during the growth process, and such failures are part of the price one pays to grow and expand one's abilities.

intelligence: A psychological concept that involves a stable difference among people in the ability to learn new things and solve challenging problems. Intelligence is measured as an IQ score in which the mean IQ is 100 and the standard deviation is 15. Therefore, 95% of the population has an IQ between 70 and 130, which are usually considered the cutoffs for intellectual dysfunction and genius, respectively.

internal versus external attributions: Internal attributions for failure suggest that your personal actions led to the failure. In contrast, external attributions suggest that the failure was due to something outside of your control.

massed practice: Trying to remember something by repeating your effort to remember it over a short period of time. The classic example of massed practice in college is the traditional "cram session" just before an exam.

spaced practice: Spreading your practice of material you are trying to learn over time (often several days or more).

stable versus unstable attributions: Stable attributions for failure assume that the cause of the failure is still present and therefore future failure in a similar situation should be expected. In contrast, unstable attributions suggest that the cause of the failure is no longer present, so whether one will fail in the future will depend on other factors.

References

Addae, J. I., Youssef, F. F., & Stone, T. W. (2003). Neuroprotective role of learning in dementia: A biologic explanation. *Journal of Alzheimer's Disease, 5*, 91-104.

Dweck, C. S. (2006). *Mindset: The new psychology of success*. New York: Ballantine Books.

Ericsson, K. A., Krampe, R. T., & Tesch-Römer, C. (1993). The role of deliberate practice in the acquisition of expert performance. *Psychological Review, 100*, 363–406. http://dx.doi.org.eps.cc.ysu.edu/10.1037/0033-295X.100.3.363.

Fogg, N., Harrington, P., Harrington, T., & Shatkin, L. (2012). *College majors handbook: The actual jobs, earnings, and trends for graduates of 50 college majors* (3rd ed). Minneapolis, MN: Jist Works.

Gazzaniga, M. S., & Mangun, G. R. (eds) (2014). *The cognitive neurosciences* (5th ed). Cambridge, MA: MIT Press.

Grobman, L., & Ramsey, E. M. (2020). *Major decisions: College, career, and the case for humanities*. Philadelphia, PA: University of Pennsylvania Press.

Kahneman, D. (2011). *Thinking, fast and slow*. New York: Farrah, Straus, and Giroux.

Kahneman, D., Sibony, O., & Sunstein, C. R. (2021). *Noise: A flaw in human judgement*. New York, NY: Little, Brown Spark.

Keengwa, J., Onchwari, G., & Oigara, J. N. (eds) (2014). *Promoting active learning through the flipped classroom model*. Hershey, PA: Information Science Reference.

Kitts, W. L. (2019). *Great jobs in the skilled trades*. San Diego, CA: Referencepoint Press.

Leahy, R. L., & Martell, C. R. (2021). *Philosophical and historical foundations. In A. Wenzel (ed), Handbook of cognitive behavioral therapy: Overview and approaches*, Vol. 1 (pp. 3-29). Washington, DC: American Psychological Association.

Love, B., Hodge, A., Corritore, C., & Ernst, D. C. (2015). Inquiry-based learning and the flipped classroom. *Problems, Resources, and Issues in Mathematics Undergraduate Studies, 25*, 745-762. https://doi.org/10.1080/10511970.2015.1046005.

Lussier, G., & Lussier, W. (2019). *Building success in the trades: Career advice for students, parents, educators, and experienced tradespeople*. Independently published on Amazon Kindle.

Mackintosh, N. J. (2011). History of theories and measurement of intelligence. In R. J. Sternberg and S. B. Kaufman (eds.), *The Cambridge handbook of intelligence* (pp. 3-19). New York, NY: Cambridge University Press.

Maquet, P. (2001). The role of sleep in learning and memory. *Science, 294*, 1048-1052. DOI: 10.1126/science.1062856.

McClelland, J. L. (2011). Memory as a constructive process: The parallel distributive processing approach. In S. Nalbantian, P. M. Matthews, & J. L. McClelland (eds), *The memory process: Neuroscientific and humanistic approaches* (pp. 129-155). Cambridge, MA: MIT Press.

McClelland, J. L., & Rumelhart, D. E. (1988). *Exploration in parallel distributed processing: A handbook of models, programs, and exercises.* Cambridge, MA: MIT Press.

Meehl, P. E. (1973). Why I do not attend case conferences. In P. E. Meehl (Ed.), *Psychodiagnosis; Selected papers* (pp. 225-302). Minneapolis, MN: University of Minnesota Press.

Mirkin, A., & Raulin, M. L. (May 2016). *The impact of student attitudes about critical thinking on student willingness to embrace such thinking.* Poster presented at the 2016 Annual Convention of the Association for Psychological Science (APS) held in Chicago.

Peterson, C., & Seligman, M. E. P. (1984). Causal explanations as a risk factor for depression: Theory and evidence. *Psychological Review, 91*(3), 347-374. http://dx.doi.org.eps.cc.ysu.edu/10.1037/0033-295X.91.3.347.

Philip, P., Taillard, J. Quera-Salva, M. A., Bioulac, B., & Akerstedt, T. (2002). Simple reaction time, duration of driving, and sleep deprivation in young versus old automobile drivers. *Journal of Sleep Research, 8*, 9-14. https://doi.org/10.1046/j.1365-2869.1999.00127.x.

Raulin, M. L., & Lilienfeld, S. O. (2015). Conducting research in the field of psychopathology. In P. Blaney, R. Kreuger, and T. Millon (eds.) *Oxford textbook of psychopathology* (3rd ed.) (pp. 100-129). New York: Oxford University Press.

Sternberg, R. J. (2015). Multiple intelligences in the new age of thinking. In S. Goldstein, D. Princiotta, and J. A. Naglieri (eds.), *Handbook of intelligence: Evolutionary theory, historical perspective, and current concepts* (pp. 229-241). New York, NY: Springer Science + Business Media.

Strunk, W. Jr., White, E. B., & Angell, R. (1999). *The elements of style* (4th Edition). Boston, MA: Pearson.

Thaler, R. H., & Sunstein, C. R. (2008). *Nudge: Improving decisions about health, wealth, and happiness.* New York, NY: Penguin Books.

Tsongas, P. (1984). *Heading Home.* New York: Knopf.

Warne, R. T. (2020). *In the know: Debunking 35 myths about human intelligence.* New York, NY: Cambridge University Press.

Warner, S. K. (2013). *Developmental influences on adult intelligence: The Seattle Longitudinal Study* (2nd Ed). New York, NY: Oxford University Press.

Williamson, P. C., & Allman, J. M. (2011). *The human illnesses: Neuropsychiatric disorders and the nature of the human brain.* New York, NY: Oxford University Press.

Wolf, K. A., & Raulin, M. L. (May, 2017). *Measuring critical thinking by having subjects evaluate the strength of arguments present in cable television show clips.* Poster presented at the Association for Psychological Science (APS) Convention in Boston.

Zinsser, W. (2016). *On writing well: The classic guide to writing nonfiction.* New York, NY: HarperCollins.

www.ingramcontent.com/pod-product-compliance
Lightning Source LLC
Chambersburg PA
CBHW050117280326
41933CB00010B/1143